SEASONS of GIVING

GIFT CRAFTING THROUGHOUT THE YEAR

By Joni Prittie

Photography by Todd Tsukushi

MEREDITH® PRESS
DES MOINES, IOWA

A WORD FROM MEREDITH® PRESS

All of us at Meredith ® Press are dedicated to offering you, our customer, the best books we can create. We are particularly concerned that all of our instructions for making projects are clear and accurate. Please address your correspondence to Customer Service Department, Meredith ® Press, Meredith Corporation, 150 East 52nd Street, New York, NY 10022.

If you would like to order additional copies of any of our books, call 1-800-678-2803 or check with your local bookstore.

Author and Designer:
Joni Prittie,
Aptos, CA

Photography:
Todd Tsukushi,
Santa Cruz, CA

Photostyling and Book Packaging:
Prittie Design,
Aptos, CA

Graphics:
Irene Morris,
Morris Design,
Monterey, CA

Illustrations:
Joni Prittie and Mike Prittie

Meredith ® Press is an imprint of Meredith ® Books:

President, Book Group:
Joseph J. Ward

Vice-President,
Editorial Director:
Elizabeth P. Rice

For Meredith ® Press:
Executive Editor:
Connie Schrader

Editorial Project Manager:
Heidi Kaisand

Copy Editor:
Carol Anderson

Proofreader:
Jennifer Miller

Production Manager:
Bill Rose

Cover Photograph:
Todd Tsukushi

Copyright © 1992 Joni Prittie
Distibuted by Meredith ®
Corporation, Des Moines, Iowa

ISBN: 0-696-02391-1
Library of Congress Catalog Number: 92-085376

Printed in the
United States of America
10 9 8 7 6 5 4 3 2 1

ACKNOWLEDGEMENTS

Come share the pleasures of creating gifts to give friends and family. As you turn the pages, you will be enchanted by the delightful crafts and charming ideas for many holiday and special occasion gifts to give throughout the year.

We at Meredith® Press strive to bring you the very highest quality craft books, with original designs, clear, easy-to-follow charts, patterns, and instructions. Each project is photographed in full color to help provide easy reference and inspiration for each project you make.

We are proud to publish "Seasons of Giving," and we hope you will enjoy using it to create your own projects, as well as gifts for others.

Sincerely,

Heidi Kaisand

Heidi Kaisand
Editorial Project Manager

From the beginning of this book project it has been clear to me that the title, *Seasons of Giving*, has many meanings. I have received so many gifts, and for these I feel so very thankful.

Merci to Ceci Powell for dear friendship and endless effort. Jodee Risney devoted her talents to creating the Golden Anniversary Memories frame, designing several gift wraps, photo-styling Summer Gift Wrap, Independence Day Gifts, Potpourri and offering general assistance wherever she could lend a hand.

Patty Schafer, Heide Merry and Julie Pain added their sewing expertise. The owners and staff of Wisteria Antiques—our beautiful location for many photographs—graciously opened their door for lovely settings and props. Paper Parade offered stunning props (some were too wonderful to return and are now in our collection). To all, so much gratitude.

To the very talented Todd Tsukushi, for patience, muffins, flawless photography, and friendship—from the bottom of my heart—thank you. Dear Irene Morris of Morris Design contributed graphic magic, many hours, and loving encouragement.

The Resource Guide at the end of the book is also a list of friends who have taken the time to support this book with great generosity of spirit. In them you will find wonderful people with beautiful offerings. Special thank yous to Paulette Knight, Beatrice Blum, John and Carolyn Grossman for inspiration and encouragement. I wish to thank Clare Gallagher, David Frym, M.I.G. McKinnon and John O. Plonk, Billie Nitz, Bill Dabney, Grace Westfield, Fred Drexler, Vicky Giese, Brad Shelton, Jan Webley, Mark Ferro, Cynthia Lenz and Sandra Cashman. Many thanks to Wendy J. Newmeyer of Main Balsam Fir Products for the Winter Woods potpourri recipe.

Thank you all for your contributions and for believing in this book. For great love, patience and devotion, Mike—more than thanks. Many, many thanks to Sharon, Ann and Susan for their support, encouragement, and love. And to you, the crafter, thank you for joining me in this renaissance of crafting as we create with our hands.

CONTENTS

INTRODUCTION

The giving and receiving of gifts is as old as remembrance. We look about our homes, filled with trinkets and treasures from those we love, and are transported to special times together.

How dearly received are the gifts we've taken time to make, for in crafting by hand, we add ingredients of care and thoughtfulness. In the quiet of creating, we gift ourselves with reflection and self-expression. *Seasons of Giving* is meant to be more than a book of projects—it has been created with the express purpose of sparking your own ideas and creativity. Many of the projects came directly from experimenting with beautiful materials, from asking "what if...?" Do not hesitate to add your favorite colors and substitute materials—we will be working hand-in-hand, for such is the art of crafting.

We begin with easy instructions for floral, ribbon, and paint techniques. The many occasions for crafting gifts—from Valentine's Day to Christmas—and the host of private reasons for celebration, including welcoming new babies, and honoring our parents are then presented. And for each occasion we offer gift ideas that you can make uniquely yours. In the last pages of the book you will find an excellent Resource Guide including materials that have been well researched for both quality and delightful service. If crafting time is short, photocopy a gift certificate and simply fill in anything from a car wash to a weekend getaway.

Over the years, I have received with great delight gifts made by friends around the world, and I have crafted gifts with joy. It feels so special to visit a friend and spy a "little something" I made long ago, quite often forgotten, displayed in a place of honor.

There are "Crafted By" labels to photocopy and add to your projects which say "Made with Love"!

I truly hope you will find great pleasure in crafting all the seasons of your life.

Joni Prittie

For Mom, Dad, and Mike

DRYING AND PRESERVING FLOWERS

Keeping a blossom's beauty has long been the dream of so many who deeply love flowers. Corsages, Valentine roses, and nosegays of spring violets are carefully tucked into special boxes to be taken out now and then for quiet daydreams.

Those of us who work with florals today are very fortunate. Developments in floral crafts have become state-of-the-art. It is delightful to discover freeze-dried gardenias and zinnias, as well as methods of preserving miniature roses and forget-me-nots. With these developments, we can achieve stunning results at home.

A large garden is not necessary in order to gather flowers and greens for crafting. Miniature roses grown on a sunny windowsill or a few pots of lavender and herbs near the doorway make wonderful materials for the crafter. A list of growers from whom to purchase materials to use for gift crafting can be found in the Resource Guide.

HARVESTING FLOWERS AND HERBS

Gather herbs and flowers for drying after the morning dew has dried completely but before the midday sun has begun to wilt them. Leave at least 2 or 3 inches of stem, and try to collect flowers in different stages of bloom. It is best to gather and dry more materials than needed to allow for breakage.

TIP FOR AIR DRYING ROSES

Enjoy cut roses as they open, and when they reach a full-blown stage, remove them from the water, cut a few inches from the stem, and hang them upside down to dry; this will ensure a better shape.

FREEZE-DRYING

Freeze-drying, one of the finest methods of food preservation, has recently been adapted to flowers. This commercial process allows for maximum retention of floral shape and color. Special machines freeze the blooms at a temperature of -30 degrees Fahrenheit for at least seven days.

Freeze-dried flowers, though delicate, are easy to work with. These flowers can even be tinted with color or accented with a wash of metallic acrylic paints.

AIR DRYING

A warm, dry area with low light is all that is required for successful drying. Special drying racks are available, but a few nails in the wall will do the job quite nicely. Simply combine 6 to 10 stems in a bundle. Secure them with string or a pretty ribbon, and hang them upside down to dry.

GLYCERIN PRESERVING

Several varieties of herbs and leaves can be preserved with glycerin purchased at the pharmacy. A mixture of two parts warm water to one part glycerin, placed in a vase or container, is absorbed by the plants. As glycerin filters into stem and leaf cells, preservation occurs. For better absorption, cut several diagonal slits in submerged stems.

PRESERVING WITH FLORAL DIPS

When flowers have been dried by one of the methods listed, floral dips may be used. They will preserve the color of the flower as dried and add flexibility. Each manufacturer of chemical floral dips provides detailed instructions on the use of its product that should be followed carefully. It is essential to work in a well-ventilated area and protect your skin during this process.

DESICCANT DRYING

Silica gel is the most reliable desiccant drying method because it allows the blooms to retain their shape and color, drying at a slow, even pace. The silica granules are quite light and will not damage delicate petals. Each manufacturer encloses instructions that should be followed carefully. The method is simple. Plastic, tin, or glass containers with airtight lids are perfect. Place flowers and leaves, evenly spaced, facing upward on a light layer of silica gel. Gently sprinkle with the silica granules until the plants are well covered. Drying flowers can be layered if containers are deep enough. Some flowers and herbs dry within six or seven days, others take longer. Experiment with times, and if you will be drying materials all summer, it is a good idea to keep notes.

A REMINDER
ABOUT OUR
RESOURCE
GUIDE

*A list of growers
from whom to
purchase materials to
use for gift crafting
can be found in the
Resource Guide
on page 162.*

PRESSING FLOWERS

Autumn leaves saved between pages of poetry... reminders of a long October walk.... Pressing flowers and leaves is the most basic method of preserving plants. Each expedition to the garden or the back lawn offers flowers and leaves for the crafter to press for notecards, gift tags, and collage work.

Common roadside greenery presses beautifully, but always check lists of endangered botanicals and poisonous plants before collecting in the wild. Mosses, berries, and single petals all press very well.

The process of pressing is uncomplicated and requires no special equipment. Large books and telephone directories work well, but once you have used a flower press, it soon becomes invaluable.

Gather the plants as they become available, and collect a large quantity to ensure a good selection while crafting. The perfect time for collecting is after the dew has evaporated and before midday, when plants are at their driest and strongest. Absorbent paper, such as blotting paper or paper toweling, is essential for this process because it absorbs moisture and oils from the plants.

SPECIAL TIP

People with known allergies should check with their physcian before handling potpourri ingredients. Occasionally essential oils and natural fixatives cause respiratory or topical reactions.

flower press is designed to exert even pressure during the process. Place several pieces of newspaper, as a base pad, on top of the bottom pressing board. *If a current paper is used, the date will indicate when pressing began to make timing easy.* Follow with absorbent paper. Lay down flowers and leaves of similar thickness, taking care not to overlap materials. Add another sheet of absorbent paper and a few sheets of newspaper. Continue layering plants and papers until all collected botanicals are in place. Secure the top pressing board and leave the plants undisturbed for a few weeks. Six weeks is a standard time for all moisture to be expressed from plants.

Gently remove pressed flowers from the press and store them between sheets of waxed paper in an airtight box or desk drawer. They should always be kept in a warm, dry place.

FLOWER TIP

To protect pressed flowers and add fragrance, brush a light coat of melted, scented wax over plant surfaces. Perfumed votive candles are perfect for this purpose. Always melt candles in a double boiler.

SPECIAL TIP

White craft glue, added with a brush to the underside of flowers and leaves, will secure materials to paper or wood.

POTPOURRI

How gentle is the art of potpourri crafting — blending color, texture, and scent on a late summer's afternoon. Nothing is wasted in the creation of a potpourri blend. Pods, leaves, fallen petals and even collected twigs and mosses become treasures. Try saving and drying petals and leaves from all the bouquets you have received during the year.

ver the centuries of using fragrant plant materials to scent our homes and ourselves, certain botanicals have proved to be true friends that always give us pleasure. Old-fashioned roses, lavender and lemon verbena give a rich base of natural scent to any potpourri mix. Calendula and sunflower petals add long-lasting colors of mellow golds and oranges to a blend, while bachelor's buttons maintain their brilliant blue. Pink rose petals usually retain their color, as do bright yellow roses, while a red rose tends to turn a deep maroon.

Textures of bark and small cones add a touch of the forest and hints of winter.

There are very few rules in the making of potpourri. Think of them as guidelines that are useful in experimentation. The essence of creating a potpourri is a threefold mix of ingredients: dried botanical materials, essential oils, and a fixative to hold the oil's scent.

Dried botanicals are accessible through growers and some health-food stores that sell bulk rosebuds and lavender as well as selections of interesting, exotic herbs and spices. When you choose materials for a potpourri, keep in mind the mood you want to create. A spring garden fragrance will require delicate colors and textures in perhaps a subtle blend of whites, pinks, and soft greens. Capture the feeling of fall with autumnal potpourri— small, colorful leaves, twigs, dried yellow roses, and mosses. A beautiful potpourri can be made by using white petals only; a combination of white roses and carnations, daisies and alyssum create a lovely bridal potpourri. Look for unusual shapes and colors. Sassafras adds a rosy brown and subtle spicy scent. Lotus and eucalyptus pods add a textural flair to woodsy potpourris.

Roses are in a category by themselves. A potpourri made by combining petals from roses of every color is absolutely breathtaking, particularly when it is scented with damask rose oil. The Fire and Ice rose makes an especially interesting potpourri, as the petals are red on one side and pure white on the other. They dry well and add a lovely touch of cream and crimson. A delicate rose potpourri can be made by using only petals from miniature roses. Modern roses are quite different from the old-fashioned varieties in that they dry well and have wonderful color but do not have the scent of old-fashioned roses.

Fixatives are a key ingredient in potpourris; they absorb and retain the volatile scented oils. If the fixative is omitted, the potpourri will quickly loose its fragrance. Fixatives can be used individually or combined. Iris germanica tubers, harvested at three years of age, dried and ground, yield orrisroot powder. Gum benzoin, oakmoss and cellulose are commonly used fixatives that are also readily available.

Creating a potpourri is as simple as mixing a few ingredients together. Gather all the materials, including a large glass or pottery bowl, a crockery cup, an eye dropper, and a small wooden spoon. (Metal and plastic are not recommended.) Be sure to keep the potpourri spoon separate from other kitchen spoons after mixing essential oils. You will need a large paper bag for seasoning potpourri and a few clothespins to seal the bag.

Measure dried botanicals following a recipe (see page 23), or invent your own pleasing combination. Mix dried petals and other botanicals in the large pottery bowl. Blend with your hands, or a wooden spoon, using gentle motions to prevent damage to petals. Set the mixture aside and place 2 to 3 tablespoons of orrisroot powder in a cup. The amount of fixative needed will be found in a recipe, however, if you are experimenting, a ratio of 2 tablespoons of fixative work well with about 4 cups of dried material. Add essential oils to fixative, 1 drop at a time, blending with a wooden spoon. The fixative should be slightly moistened but not saturated with oils. Add the scented fixative to the dried materials. Place the mixture in a paper bag and seal the top with clothespins or clips. Turn the bag over several times to distribute the fixative. Store the bag away from direct sunlight and allow the mix to season for four to six weeks.

FLOWERS, HERBS AND PETALS

Color and fragrance abound in the garden, waiting to be collected for potpourri crafting. Be sure to dry citrus peel and berries thoroughly before using in a potpourri. To add a touch of the sea, place a few tiny shells from a special beach in your potpourri.

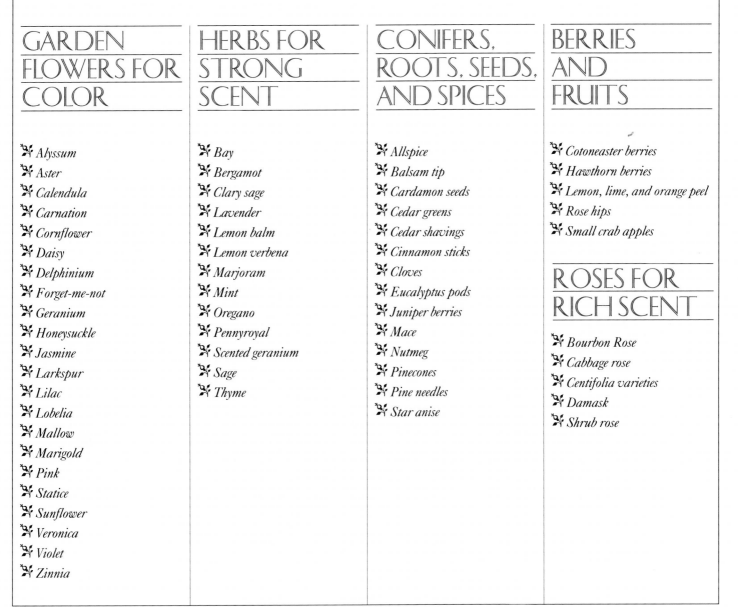

GARDEN FLOWERS FOR COLOR

- Alyssum
- Aster
- Calendula
- Carnation
- Cornflower
- Daisy
- Delphinium
- Forget-me-not
- Geranium
- Honeysuckle
- Jasmine
- Larkspur
- Lilac
- Lobelia
- Mallow
- Marigold
- Pink
- Statice
- Sunflower
- Veronica
- Violet
- Zinnia

HERBS FOR STRONG SCENT

- Bay
- Bergamot
- Clary sage
- Lavender
- Lemon balm
- Lemon verbena
- Marjoram
- Mint
- Oregano
- Pennyroyal
- Scented geranium
- Sage
- Thyme

CONIFERS, ROOTS, SEEDS, AND SPICES

- Allspice
- Balsam tip
- Cardamon seeds
- Cedar greens
- Cedar shavings
- Cinnamon sticks
- Cloves
- Eucalyptus pods
- Juniper berries
- Mace
- Nutmeg
- Pinecones
- Pine needles
- Star anise

BERRIES AND FRUITS

- Cotoneaster berries
- Hawthorn berries
- Lemon, lime, and orange peel
- Rose hips
- Small crab apples

ROSES FOR RICH SCENT

- Bourbon Rose
- Cabbage rose
- Centifolia varieties
- Damask
- Shrub rose

ESSENTIAL OILS AND THEIR USES

Essential oils can be obtained in a pure, botanical form or commercially blended for use.
Blending scents is a wonderful experience, and experimentation will soon yield a delightful perfume.
Blend oils together, drop by drop, until the mix is pleasing. Record your favorite blends, as you may wish
to re-create them. ❧ Scents can be categorized as floral, herbal, citrus, spicy, woodsy, or exotic.
Oils that create different moods can be blended beautifully. Begin with a predominant scent,
then add complementary oils drop by drop.

FLORAL

- *Damask rose*
- *French lilac*
- *French rose*
- *Honeysuckle*
- *Jasmine*
- *Lavender*
- *Lily of the Valley*
- *Rose*
- *Tuberose*

HERBAL

- *Basil*
- *Peppermint*
- *Rosemary*
- *Sage*
- *Thyme*

CITRUS

- *Lemon*
- *Lemongrass*
- *Lime*
- *Orange*
- *Tangerine*

SPICE

- *Allspice*
- *Bitter almond*
- *Cinnamon*
- *Cloves*
- *Vanilla*

WOODSY

- *Cedar*
- *Cypress*
- *Juniper*
- *Rosewood*
- *Sandalwood*
- *White pine*

EXOTIC

- *Amber*
- *Frankincense*
- *Myrrh*
- *Patchouli*

POTPOURRI RECIPES

Recipes for potpourri are just the beginning of the enjoyment of creating scented gifts. Whether materials are grown and gathered, or purchased from a grower, it soon becomes evident that the combinations of florals are endless and experimenting is extrememly enjoyable.

SPRING MORNING

2 cups pink rosebuds

1 cup blue malva petals

^{1}/$_2$ cup green leaves

1 cup pink larkspur

1 cup lavender

1 cup white petals

4 tablespoons orrisroot powder

6 drops French lilac oil

2 drops honeysuckle oil

1 drop damask oil

1 drop lemongrass oil

VICTORIAN SUMMER ROSE

2 cups pink rose petals

2 cups white rose petals

1 cup red rose petals

2 cups rose leaves

1 cup rosebuds, pink or red

2 cups baby's breath florets

7 tablespoons orrisroot powder

12 drops damask or French rose oil

AUTUMN HARVEST

2 cups calendula petals

2 cups yellow rose petals

2 cups oakmoss

1 cup sandalwood chips

1 cup lemon verbena

1 cup orange peel

5 tablespoons orrisroot powder

3 drops ylang-ylang

2 drops sweet orange oil

3 drops patchouli oil

WINTER WOODS

3 cups balsam fir tips

1 cup rosebuds and petals

^{1}/$_2$ cup lavender blossoms

^{1}/$_2$ cup lemon or orange peel

^{1}/$_2$ cup oakmoss

1 teaspoon whole cloves

1 teaspoon whole allspice

2 tablespoons orrisroot

Few drops essential oil (balsam suggested)

RIBBONS AND TRIMS

Ribbons of satin and silk, Irish lace, and tiny Victorian charms of brass add lovely details to gifts. Many types of trims are available and each has a place in the crafter's basket.

RIBBONS

Silk ribbons have been wired in France for well over 100 years, especially in the Midi, near the city of Lyons. Wired ribbons are especially easy to handle and give the most beautiful effects. The French wired ribbons used in the gift projects in *Seasons of Giving* have been woven by hand on original looms in the most subtle colors, with gold and silver edges and various motifs. Ribbon is also being wired in the United States in lovely shades and patterns.

Antique-silk ribbons are of the lightest-weight silk in soft, rich colors, for fine detailing. Small roses of antique-silk ribbons are especially good trims for baby gifts and other delicate crafting.

Hand-painted ribbons of rayon and silk are works of art. Delicately marbled patterns of soft tones and rich colors make these ribbons simply irresistible. This special ribbon is available through the supplier listed in the Resource Guide.

Hand paint ribbons at home by experimenting with acrylic paints mixed with water. Moisten ribbon first and dot on washes of paint (see page 33). Color should bleed into ribbon fibers for interesting effects.

Paper ribbons, especially suitable for wreaths and baskets, are available in every color imaginable. Try "painting" on a deep jewel-tone paper ribbon with liquid bleach. The effect is that of tone-on-tone batik fabric.

Tea-dyed ribbon and lace have an aged look that is appropriate for a Victorian flavor. Brew a strong pot of tea using 3 or 4 teabags. Allow tea to cool slightly. Dip ribbons or lace into tea and check for color saturation. A mottled effect is created by bunching ribbon tightly and securing with a rubberband. Allow ribbon to dry completely before removing band. To ensure good quality dyeing, always test a small piece of ribbon or lace before dyeing large amounts.

GLOSSARY OF RIBBON TERMS

ANTIQUE: *Authentic or reproduction ribbons from past centuries.*

BROCADE: *Heavyweight silk or woven, figured, or floral ribbon; in some instances metallic threads are incorporated.*

CHIFFON: *Exceedingly fine-textured, soft, lightweight taffeta.*

GROSGRAIN: *Ribbon of ribbed fabric with the heaviest thread running crosswise.*

IRIDESCENT: *The weave of a ribbon that gives a rainbow effect; as the ribbon is moved, the colors of the prism appear.*

JACQUARD: *The weave of a ribbon that gives an intricate, variegated pattern.*

MOIRÉ: *The weave of a ribbon that creates a water effect.*

MOTIF: *The units of a design that are repeated in a pattern.*

OMBRÉ: *The weave of a ribbon that gives a shaded effect.*

ORGANDY: *A soft, thin, transparent ribbon of silk, cotton or rayon.*

SATIN: *Silk with a close weave, resulting in a glossy, rich effect.*

TAFFETA: *An extremely fine-textured, smooth silk that is one of the oldest weaves.*

VELVET: *Silk that is often woven on a cotton back with thick pile.*

WIRED: *Ribbon woven with wire edges (the wire is treated as a thread when weaving) that is used to hold a shape for bows and twists.*

GLUE FOR RIBBONS AND TRIMS

he glue gun is indispensable for crafting. Most gifts in *Seasons of Giving* were made with a hot glue gun. A low-temperature glue and glue gun are also available. These work particularly well on foil trims, and other light materials that often melt when secured with hot glue.

White craft glue, or fabric glue, applied to fine cords and braids with a small brush will secure trims to the edges of pillows and boxes. Be sure to wash the glue from the brush frequently, as hardened glue damages bristles.

Charms and buttons can be secured in place with glue made expressly for metal and porcelain.

See the Resource Guide for an excellent source of this glue.

BOWS

Instructions for single bow will make a single bow with an overall width of 5½ inches with two 4½-inch long streamers.

SINGLE BOW

STEP 1
Cut one yard of ribbon into one 20-inch piece to use for loops and one 16-inch piece to use for streamers.

STEP 2
Using the 20-inch length, form a loop of desired fullness with ribbon held firmly between thumb and index finger (see illustration 1).

illustration 1

STEP 3
Holding bow center, twist ribbon and form a second loop opposite the first. Secure center with a twist of wire (see illustration 2).

illustration 2

Ribbon loop ends will be trimmed after streamers are added.

STEP 4
To make bow streamers, tie remaining ribbon length around bow center (see illustrations 3 and 4). Trim away ribbon loop ends. Trim bow streamers to desired length and shape (see illustration 5).

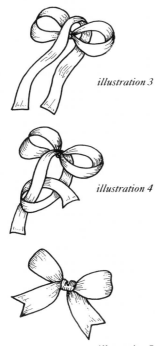

illustration 3

illustration 4

illustration 5

DOUBLE/FULLER BOWS

Follow the steps for creating a single bow, making the length used for bow loops twice as long for a double bow, or three times as long for a triple bow. After second bow loop is formed, twist ribbon to form a loop on top of the first loop. Working from side to side, twist and loop ribbon until a bow of desired fullness is formed. Secure center with a twist of wire.

LADDER BOW

A variation of a decorative bow used in Victorian millinery, this chain of single bows is both great fun to tie and useful to adorn basket handles and glue to barrettes. Ladder bows are quite pretty to wear with French-braided hair. These instructions will make a ladder bow 3 inches wide overall and 4 inches long.

STEP 1
Cut one 3-yard length of ribbon.

STEP 2
First bow should be tied at center point of ribbon length (see illustrations 6, 7 and 8).

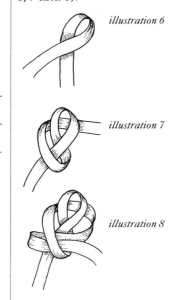

illustration 6

illustration 7

illustration 8

Tie a single knot after each bow (see illustration 9). After tying knot, adjust bow loops and tighten knot.

illustration 9

STEP 3

Tie another single bow, a knot, and continue with this pattern of bows and knots until the needed length of bow chain is formed. (see illustration 10).

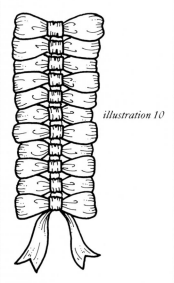

illustration 10

STEP 4

Trim streamers to the desired length.

RIBBON ROSES

Ribbon roses are easily fashioned from wired ribbon. Both ruffled roses and old-fashioned roses can be created for wraps and trims.

RUFFLED ROSE

STEP 1

Cut one 24-inch piece of wired ribbon. Fold one end of ribbon over itself about ¼ inch, pressing hard to secure wire (see illustration 11).

illustration 11

STEP 2

Gently pull one wire from the opposite end, gathering the ribbon as you go. Pull approximately 9 inches of wire through (see illustration 12).

illustration 12

STEP 3

Roll pulled wire section to form a rose. (see illustration 13)

illustration 13

Finish rose by twisting extended wire around the base of the ruffled ribbon several times to secure (see illustrations 14 and 15).

illustration 14   *illustration 15*

Large open roses can be fashioned by using wired ribbon with a width of 2 or more inches.

OLD-FASHIONED ROSE

STEP 1

Cut one 12-inch piece of wired ribbon. Fold ribbon end at right angle to ribbon edge (see illustration 16). Roll folded end in tightly to form rose center.

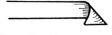

illustration 16

STEP 2

Fold ribbon length back over itself (away from yourself) forming an elongated triangle (see illustration 17). Continue folding ribbon along each new fold line until folded section has been rolled in (see illustration 18).

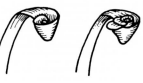

illustration 17   *illustration 18*

STEP 3

Continue folding and rolling until rose is desired size. A twist of craft wire will hold rose base in place.

RUFFLES AND FRILLS

Create ribbon ruffles and frills by tightly folding over one end of French wired ribbon length to secure, then pulling one or both wires from opposite end to create a ruffle or a double-gathered frill (also known as ruching).

RIBBON KNOTS AND BRAIDS

Ribbons need not be limited to use as bows for decorating. A length of ribbon, tied in loose, single knots, makes a wonderful trim for baskets and boxes. Ribbon can be knotted at 1- or 2-inch intervals; the knots will resemble rosettes. Small loops of green ribbon can be glued beneath each knot rosette to form leaves.

Braiding ribbons enables the crafter to design custom trimmings. Three equal lengths of ribbon braided together create tailored trimmings. Substitute lace, metallic ribbon or metallic cord for one of the ribbon lengths to form an unusual gift trim.

LACE

Laces made of natural and synthetic fibers are readily available in a wide variety of patterns and widths. Natural-fiber laces can be tea-dyed (see page 24), and will accept washes of acrylic paint for delicate coloring (see page 33). Crisp Battenberg lace can also be tea-dyed for Victorian crafting. Ruffled lace and lace woven with a pull string for gathering can be used to edge baskets and boxes.

TRIMS

Tassels, cords, braids, and buttons are trims every crafter finds useful. Available through fabric or craft shops, the selection will suit every taste and budget. A supplier for most unusual and delicate European trims can be found in the Resource Guide. Sterling silver and pewter buttons add an heirloom touch to projects and gifts.

TASSELS

Tassels, custom-coordinated to projects, can be made easily and inexpensively with thread by following these directions. Silk and rayon threads are recommended for this purpose. Subtle colors and metallics can be used together for jewelry tassels and Victorian Christmas crafting.

MATERIALS:

One or more spools silk or rayon thread (6 or 7 threads wound together facilitate the work)

3x5-inch file card or piece of cardboard

10 inches fine craft wire or thin gold elastic cord

Small, sharp scissors

STEP 1
Tie one end of threads together in a knot. Holding thread ends against file card, wind around card until tassel is desired thickness. Keep in mind that thickness will include thread on both sides of card.

STEP 2
Cut wire or cord in half, slipping one piece under threads at top of card. Twist wire or tie cord to secure.

STEP 3
Cut threads along bottom edge of card and pull tassel up and away from card.

STEP 4
Use remaining wire or cord to wind around tassel approximately ¼ inch from top. Trim tassel ends to desired length. Top wire or cord can be used to attach tassel to projects.

BOUILLON "CRINKLE" WIRE

European bouillon wire, produced for more than 100 years, is a thin, spirally wound wire that is available in silver and gold. Bouillon wire can be stretched quite long to create strong, fine threads of metallic rickrack to add glistening detail to projects, jewelry, and gift wrap. A supplier for this exquisite trim is listed in the Resource Guide.

JOHN LINE & SONS LTD
PURE DAGGER HAIR
6½

PAINT TECHNIQUES

Blues of the summer sky, peach tulips blooming among pale yellow hyacinths...we are surrounded by the inspiration of color. Painting is the most self-expressive of art forms—we mix colors, apply hues and, with the stroke of a brush, transform simple things into objects of delight.

 Fundamental paint techniques are easy to master. The methods listed in this section are used in the gift projects which follow, and can be easily adapted to larger items. Exploring color and paint application is an adventure for beginners and experts alike.

The paint used for projects was exclusively acrylic-based due to the ease of application and simple clean-up. Acrylic paints dry quickly and are available in vast color selections, including a wide range of metallic colors.

PROTECTION FOR PAINTED SURFACES

Acrylic paint is both durable and non-fading but if a project, such as a birdhouse, is to be used outdoors, a protective coat of varnish is desirable. Varnishes are available in a high-gloss finish, as well as a softer, satin finish. Apply two or three thin, even coats and allow each coat to dry completely before adding another.

RAGGING COLORS

The ragging technique produces an uneven pattern of shapes.

MATERIALS:

Small, soft rags of natural fiber

Water

Bowls for mixing paints

Watercolor brush for mixing paints and applying base coat

2 or 3 complementary colors of acrylic paints

STEP 1

Using brush, apply base coat of acrylic paint. Allow paint to dry completely.

STEP 2

Moisten soft rag with water, wring out excess. Dip rag in complementary paint color and wring out excess. (Full-strength paint can be ragged, or paint can be thinned with water for a softer pattern effect.) Crumple rag, place on surface. Using both hands, roll rag over surface. Repeat procedure as often as necessary to cover entire surface. Allow paint to dry completely if a third color is to be ragged. Seal with varnish if desired (see page 31).

RAGGING IDEA

Try ragging violet on a base coat of metallic silver paint, followed by a second ragging of teal for an especially lustrous effect.

SPONGING

The sponging technique produces a flecked, broken pattern, less bold than ragging. Sponging has more depth when three colors are combined.

MATERIALS:

Natural sea sponge, or pieces of sponge for small projects

Water

Bowl for mixing paint colors

Watercolor brush for mixing paint and applying base coat

2 or 3 complementary colors of acrylic paint

STEP 1

Using brush, apply base coat of acrylic paint. Allow paint to dry completely.

STEP 2

Moisten sponge with water and wring out excess. Lightly dip sponge in paint bowl. (Full strength paint can be sponged, or thinned with water for softer pattern effect.) Touch sponge to surface. Change direction now and then for a more uneven pattern. Allow paint to dry completely if a third coat is to be sponged. Seal with varnish if desired (see page 31).

A NOTE ON COLORS

Metallics sponge well—try a copper base coat with sponging of metallic gold and soft turquoise for the effect of antique copper

CRACKLING

The crackling paint technique produces a most interesting antique effect, as if paint has aged for years. It has been made easy by the development of new synthetic (non-animal based) products.
The Resource Guide lists the manufacturer of an excellent crackle medium.

MATERIALS:

Crackle medium

Watercolor brush, for base coat and crackle

Two colors of acrylic paint

CRACKLE COLOR IDEAS

Crackle picture frames and small baskets with a dusty rose base coat and an antique white or cream top coat.

STEP 1
Using brush, apply base coat of acrylic paint. Allow to dry completely.

STEP 2
Using brush, apply an even coat of clear crackle medium. Allow this coat to dry and set completely (follow manufacturer's suggestions as crackle mediums differ.)

STEP 3
Apply a coat of another color. As this coat dries, the paint will crackle, and base color will be exposed. Seal with varnish if desired (see page 31).

FABRIC PAINTING

MATERIALS:

Fabric or clothing item

Cardboard piece slightly larger than design to be painted

Watercolor brush

Acrylic paint

Squeeze-bottle fabric paint (optional)

STEP 1
Wash and dry fabric or clothing item to remove sizing. Iron if necessary.

STEP 2
Transfer design to fabric (see page 34). Place cardboard under fabric area to be painted.

STEP 3
Using brush, apply acrylic paint to larger design areas. Use squeeze-bottle paint for outlines and details.

COLOR WASHES

MATERIALS:

Water

Bowl for mixing

Watercolor brush

Acrylic paint

STEP 1
Mix a small amount of paint with water in a jar or bowl. The more water added, the lighter the wash, and the less defined the color.

STEP 2
Apply wash using quick, free brush strokes. Seal with varnish if desired (see page 34).

PAINTING BRASS CHARMS

Brass, when left to the elements, will darken naturally. Acrylic paints work beautifully on prepared charms to create an antique or enamel effect.

MATERIALS:

Ethyl alcohol or rubbing alcohol
Cotton ball
Paper towels
Acrylic paint
Watercolor brush
Varnish

STEP 1
Using cotton ball, apply alcohol to the brass charms to prepare the surface to receive paint. Dry thoroughly.

STEP 2
Using brush, apply acrylic paint. With paper towel, wipe away excess paint. Some paint will remain in the crevices, creating an aged effect. For an enameled look, do not wipe away excess paint.

STEP 3
Seal charms with varnish when dry.

TRANSFERRING PATTERNS TO FABRIC

MATERIALS:

Tracing paper
Fine-tipped iron-on transfer pens
Iron

STEP 1
Place tracing paper on design to be transferred. Use one or several colors of fine-tipped iron-on transfer pens to trace design.

STEP 2
Place traced design, ink side down, on fabric and apply pre-heated iron (follow transfer pen manufacturer's suggestions). Press iron rather than sliding it, to prevent the design from becoming blurred. Leave paper in place for a few seconds so design can cool, then remove.

TRANSFERRING PATTERNS TO PAPER OR WOOD

MATERIALS:

Tracing paper
Medium-hard lead pencil
Soft lead pencil
Low tack tape

STEP 1
Trace pattern to be copied using medium-hard lead pencil. Draw over all design lines onto tracing paper.

STEP 2
Using soft lead pencil, shade back of traced design.

STEP 3
Place paper, shaded side down, on surface where design is desired. Using low tack tape, secure in place.

STEP 4
Using medium-hard pencil, redraw design. Design will transfer to surface.

ENLARGING PATTERNS

MATERIALS:

Ruler
Large sheet of paper
Pencil or pen

Refer to scale figures near printed pattern to determine enlarged pattern measurements (i.e. one square equals one inch). Using a pencil or pen and ruler, draw a grid of squares on paper large enough to accommodate enlarged measurements. Copy the pattern onto drawn grid. To facilitate copying, copy lines of printed pattern one square at a time.

BRUSHES FOR GIFT CRAFTING

Brushes selected for crafting were chosen for use with acrylic paints. Synthetic bristle brushes clean easily and resist breakage. Acrylic paint may actually damage natural hair brushes if they are not cleaned immediately.

ROUND BRUSH

illustration 19

A round tip allows the brush to go from a thick to a thin line, depending on how much pressure is applied. This is a versatile brush tip for general painting.

LINER BRUSH

illustration 20

The liner brush is used for fine detail and outlines. This brush consists of a small number of bristles placed in a round-tip configuration.

SHADER BRUSH

illustration 21

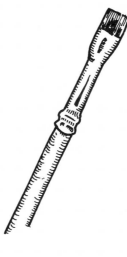

The shader brush is used to apply a base coat and fill in color areas. The flattened bristle area with sharp edges allows the crafter to be precise in applying paint.

FAN BRUSH

illustration 22

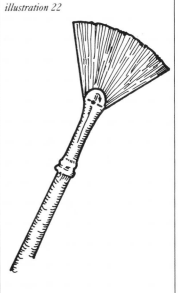

The fan brush is used for blending colors and creating thin, even coats of paint. Light strokes with a fan brush will add a few thin lines of color for a soft, antiquing effect.

VALENTINE'S DAY

The secret of any gift is surely a generous heart. Gifts made with love need not be large or expensive: it is the care of the crafter's hand that reaches out in all we make. Let us take more time this year to give of ourselves, to shower love on family and friends. Valentine's Day is the perfect time to begin.

Create a simple heart of heavenly lavender for someone special. If there is room in the garden for lavender plants, you will find an ample supply of flowers for an entire year of crafting. How special to share the garden with those who are dear to us.

VALENTINE WREATH OF LAVENDER

MATERIALS:

One 7-inch-wide heart-shaped twig wreath

1 bunch dried lavender

1 white rose, dried, freeze-dried, or silk

2 sprigs small silk lilac blossoms

3 sprigs dried green fern

1¼ yards of ½-inch-wide soft pink French wired ribbon

2 lengths gold bouillon wire

Scissors

Glue gun/glue sticks

STEP 1
Trim stems from lavender spikes. Place wreath on flat surface and glue lavender spikes, pointing downward to cover wreath front.

STEP 2
Glue white rose to wreath at heart center, encircling rose with silk flowers and fern leaves.

STEP 3
Cut one 5-inch piece of French wired ribbon. To form hanger, place ribbon ends on back of rounded shapes of heart. With hot glue, secure ribbon to heart.

STEP 4
Use remaining ribbon to tie a single bow with two streamers (see page 27). Trim streamer ends in an inverted "V" shape. Glue bow to ribbon hanger at topmost point.

STEP 5
Pull gold bouillon wire to lengthen and create a rickrack pattern (see page 29). Wrap wire around center of bow several times, leaving gold streamers twirling from center of bow. Use remaining wire to loop in and out around rose.

HEARTS AND FLOWERS PILLOW

MATERIALS:

Two 8x8-inch squares deep plum soft, fine-textured fabric

⅔ yard of gold, maroon and red satin metallic cord

⅓ yard of ⅛-inch-wide antique gold metallic cord

¼ yard of ½-inch-wide gold metallic gimp braid

5 inches of 1-inch-wide lilac French wired ribbon

4 spikes dried lavender

1 small preserved rose

Cotton batting

Small amount dried lavender

Coordinating thread and needle

Glue gun/glue sticks

STEP 1

Enlarge and transfer pattern, illustration 23, to wrong side of fabric (see page 34). Cut out two hearts.

STEP 2

Put right sides of fabric together and stitch ¼ inch from raw edge, leaving 2 or 3 inches open for stuffing. Cut slits along curves to ease fabric. Turn right side out. With cotton batting, stuff to desired firmness. Add dried lavender to the batting. Slip-stitch opening closed (see illustration 24).

illustration 24

STEP 3

Glue metallic gimp braid into place, beginning at center of one heart curve and ending diagonally on opposite side, just above heart point. Glue satin metallic cord around heart pillow, beginning and ending at heart indentation.

STEP 4

Using wired ribbon, tie a single knot around lavender spikes. Trim streamer ends in an inverted "V" shape. Glue ribbon and lavender to center of gimp braid. Glue preserved rose to center of knot. Tie single bow of metallic cord (see page 27). Glue bow to heart indentation.

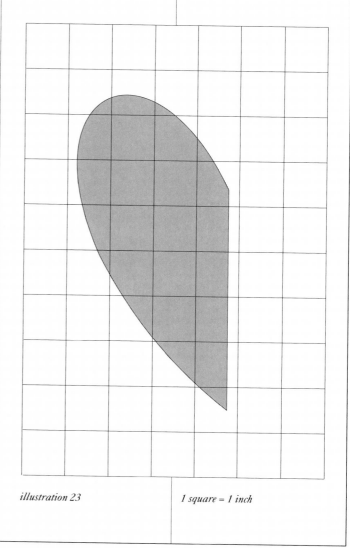

illustration 23   *1 square = 1 inch*

VICTORIAN VALENTINE PILLOW

MATERIALS:

Two 9x9-inch squares iridescent rosy violet raw silk

¾ yard of 1/16-inch-wide silver metallic cord

¼ yard of 1½-inch-wide hunter green organdy ribbon

Metallic gold, emerald and royal purple silk or rayon thread for bow

One 2x3-inch embroidered silver braid medallion

Light blue acrylic paint

1 small cherub-shaped brass charm

1 small heart-shaped brass locket charm

1 brass filigree charm spacer

10-12 small red and pink preserved rosebuds

Small amount gold wire

3x5-inch index card

Cotton batting

Glue gun/glue sticks

STEP 1

Enlarge and transfer pattern, illustration 25, to wrong side of fabric (see page 34). Cut out two hearts. Antique charms using light blue acrylic paint (see page 34).

STEP 2

Put right sides of fabric together and stitch ¼ inch from raw edge, leaving 2 or 3 inches open for stuffing. Cut slits along curve to ease fabric. Turn right side out. With cotton batting, stuff pillow to desired firmness. (Potpourri may be added to batting to scent pillow.) Slip-stitch opening closed (see illustration 26).

illustration 26

STEP 3

Glue silver metallic cord around heart-shaped pillow, beginning and ending at heart indentation.

STEP 4

Form a double bow of organdy ribbon, approximately 3 inches wide overall, no streamers (see page 27). Secure center of bow with craft wire.

STEP 5

Tie thread ends together in a knot. Holding thread ends against file card wind thread around card to desired thickness. Do not cut thread. Carefully slip thread off card. Secure in center with craft wire, creating a bow of thread. Attach to center of organdy bow with craft wire.

STEP 6

Attach charm spacer to bow lengthwise with craft wire. Attach heart-shaped locket to bottom of spacer with wire. Glue cherub-shaped charm to bow, centering over spacer. Glue one rosebud to center of spacer. Glue remaining rosebuds around cherub-shaped charm.

STEP 7

Glue silver braid medallion to center of heart pillow just below indentation. Glue bow with charms across heart indentation.

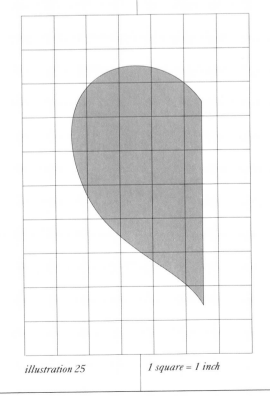

illustration 25   *1 square = 1 inch*

VALENTINE KEEPSAKE BOX

MATERIALS:

3³⁄₄x4x2-inch heart-shaped wooden box

Lilac, grape, deep rose and metallic gold acrylic paint

Shader brush

1 piece light poster board

Cotton batting

Small piece antique rose soft, fine-textured fabric

¹⁄₂ yard of ¹⁄₂-inch-wide burgundy braid with tassels

1 yard of ¹⁄₄-inch-wide plum rayon soutache

4 preserved red miniature roses

1 yard of gold metallic thread

1 yard of metallic magenta thread

1 yard deep rose thread

One 2¹⁄₂x2¹⁄₂-inch piece cardboard for making tassels

Pencil

Scissors

Glue gun/glue sticks

STEP 1

Paint interior of box with gold paint. Allow paint to dry completely.

STEP 2

Paint box exterior, except top of box with lilac paint. Allow paint to dry completely.

STEP 3

Sponge deep rose paint onto painted surfaces, creating a pleasing pattern (see page 32). Sponge additional layers of grape and gold paint, allowing paint to dry completely between coats.

STEP 4

Place top of box on poster board and draw around shape with pencil. Cut out and lay poster-board heart on batting. Cut batting to exact size. Set batting heart aside.

STEP 5

Place poster board heart-shaped pattern on fabric and draw around it with a pencil. Cut heart shape 1 inch larger on all sides so extra fabric can be turned under.

STEP 6

Cut ⁵⁄₈-inch notches around fabric heart edges at 2-inch intervals.

STEP 7

Glue batting to poster board heart. Place fabric heart on table, right side down. Center poster board heart, batting side down, on top of fabric. Working in sections, glue notched fabric edges to smooth side of poster board. Glue padded fabric heart to top of box.

STEP 8

Glue burgundy braid with tassels around side of box top beginning and ending at heart indentation. Glue rayon soutache to upper edge of braid, beginning and ending at heart inden-tation, and overlapping onto fabric.

STEP 9

Using the gold, magenta, and deep rose threads and the piece of cardboard make a silk thread tassel (see page 29). Glue top of tassel to top of box, 1 inch below heart indentation.

STEP 10

With hot glue, attach roses to box top near heart indentation. Finish box by gluing soutache to lower edge of bottom of box, beginning and ending at heart indentation.

For
Valentine's Day,
or for any day
of the year, make a
token of your love
for a best friend
to cherish.

VALENTINE DIARY

MATERIALS:

One 4x6½-inch notebook

12x8½-inch small floral print cotton fabric

4x4-inch square of lace

1 brass heart-shaped charm

1 brass bird-shaped charm

1½ yards of ⅛-inch-wide dusty rose antique silk grosgrain ribbon

1 dried pink rosebud

Blue acrylic paint

Liner brush

Tracing paper

Gold craft wire

Pinking or scalloping shears

Fabric glue

Glue gun/glue sticks

STEP 1

Using liner brush, paint bird-shaped charm with blue paint and seal (see page 34). Seal heart-shaped locket (see page 34). Set charm and locket aside to dry.

STEP 2

Fold fabric, ironing folds into place according to illustration 27. Glue with fabric glue to secure. Slip book into cover.

STEP 3

Trace heart-shaped pattern, illustration 28, onto tracing paper. Cut out. Fold lace square in half. Place heart-shaped pattern on top of lace with center line on fold. Cut heart-shaped pattern out of lace. With fabric glue attach lace to front of book.

STEP 4

Using grosgrain ribbon, tie a 10-loop full bow, approximately 2½ inches wide overall, with four streamers (see page 27).

STEP 5

Wire rosebud to bird-shaped charm's back. With hot glue, attach bird to center of bow. With hot glue, attach heart-shaped locket to book cover directly below bird-shaped charm. With hot glue, attach bow to top of lace heart.

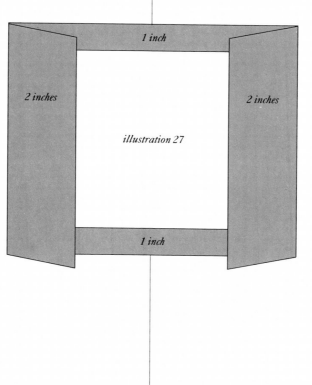

1 inch

2 inches   2 inches

illustration 27

1 inch

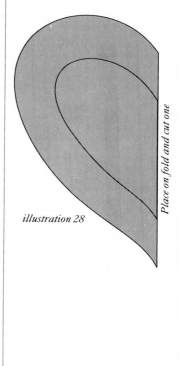

illustration 28

Place on fold and cut one

The sweetness of the rose, the spice of cinnamon, and the herbal richness of sweet Annie are bundled together to scent a writing desk or shelf. Tie your gift in a favorite color of French ribbon to say "Je t'aime" ("I love you".)

CINNAMON AND ROSES

MATERIALS:

Forty 4-inch cinnamon sticks

16 large dried or freeze-dried rosebuds

40 sprigs sweet Annie, approximately 3 inches long

1¼ yards of 1-inch-wide color range of navy, plum, raspberry, light blue and lime French wired ombré ribbon

Glue gun/glue sticks

STEP 1
Glue cinnamon stick sides together one by one to create a bundle. Stand sticks on flat surface while gluing so finished bundle will be freestanding. Make sure outer sides of bundle have no glue showing.

STEP 2
Glue 7 to 8 rosebuds to the tops of cinnamon sticks around outer edge.
To build the dome shape, glue rosebuds to sides and backs of rosebuds already in place, working in a circular pattern.

STEP 3
Glue sprigs of sweet Annie in gaps among the roses.

STEP 4
Cut enough ribbon to encircle cinnamon stick bundle. Glue into place around cinnamon bundle. With remaining ribbon, tie a pretty double bow (see page 27). Glue bow into place at front of bundle.

SWEET HEART OF ROSES

MATERIALS:

One 5x4x2-inch heart-shaped box

Deep rose acrylic paint

Shader brush

1 cup Victorian Summer Rose potpourri (see recipe, page 23)

4 to 5 spikes dried lavender

1/2 yard of 3/4-inch sage floral jacquard ribbon

1/2 yard of 2-inch-wide rose organdy ribbon

1/2 yard of 3/8-inch-wide metallic picot trim with peach ribbon

25 to 35 dried deep pink rosebuds

3 yards of 1/4-inch-wide cranberry antique silk ribbon

1 brass cherub-shaped charm

White craft glue

Glue suitable for metal

Glue gun/glue sticks

STEP 1
Paint exterior of heart-shaped box bottom with deep rose paint. Allow paint to dry completely.

STEP 2
Pour craft glue into box to a thickness of approximately ¼ inch. With this glue, completely cover the interior sides of the box. While glue is wet, place potpourri into box, covering sides and bottom of interior completely. Add extra potpourri as needed to cover interior.

STEP 3
Add lavender spikes and a few whole rosebuds to potpourri to create a small arrangement. Allow glue to set before proceeding.

STEP 4
With hot glue, attach organdy ribbon around box exterior, beginning and ending at center point of heart indentation. With glue placed at beginning, lower heart point and ribbon end will be secure.

STEP 5
Center jacquard ribbon on organdy ribbon. With hot glue, attach jacquard ribbon to organdy ribbon. With hot glue, attach picot trim around top outside edge of box.

STEP 6
With hot glue, attach dried rosebuds around top edge of box (stems can be glued to box interior), facing upward to create a rosebud frame.

STEP 7
Cut one 4-inch piece of cranberry antique silk ribbon. To form hanger, place ribbon ends at topmost points of heart's curves. With hot glue, secure ribbon to heart. Cut remaining cranberry antique silk ribbon in half. Make two 6-loop bows with several streamers (see page 27). With hot glue, attach bows to cover ends of ribbon hanger. With glue for metal, attach cherub-shaped charm to topmost point of ribbon hanger.

FRIENDSHIP GARDEN PIN

MATERIALS:

1 double cherub-shaped brass charm

1 tiny heart-shaped brass charm

1 heart-shaped brass locket

1 flower basket-shaped brass charm

1 brass filigree charm spacer

1 pinback

Metallic gold, blue, red and green acrylic paint

Thin brass craft wire

¼ yard of 1½-inch-wide rose organdy ribbon

3 to 5 dried rosebuds

Wire cutter

Glue suitable for metal

Glue gun/glue sticks

STEP 1
Prepare charms (see page 34).

STEP 2
Cut six 4-inch lengths of wire. Thread one wire through left-hand loop on bottom edge of filigree charm spacer. Pull wire through until ends meet. Thread both wire ends through top loop of locket charm, one wire end through back of loop, and one wire through front of loop. Adjust locket position to approximately ½ inch from spacer and tightly twist wire ends around the wire length between spacer and charm. Press wire ends into this twist so there are no sharp ends exposed. A stiff ½-inch hanger will result.

STEP 3
Repeat Step 2 to hang flower basket-shaped charm on lower center loop of spacer and tiny heart-shaped charm on right-hand lower loop of spacer.

STEP 4
Cut one 5-inch piece of ribbon. Make a single bow, securing center of bow with a twist of wire (see page 27). Use remaining ribbon to form a smaller single bow, secured with a twist of wire.

STEP 5
With glue for metal, attach double cherub-shaped brass charm to center of large bow.

STEP 6
Thread remaining 4-inch piece of wire through top hole of filigree charm spacer and twist ends around center of small bow, with spacer and charms hanging behind and below bow.

STEP 7
With hot glue, secure small bow to large bow below cherub-shaped brass charm.

STEP 8
With hot glue, attach rosebuds to top and center of small bow. This will cover any glue that shows when bows are glued together. With hot glue, attach pinback to back of large bow.

MON AMIE

MATERIALS:

1 cherub-shaped brass charm

Blue acrylic paint

½ yard of 1-inch-wide celery green French wired ribbon

Gold, copper, silver, and variegated metallic silk or rayon thread for tassels

Thin brass craft wire

5 small dried deep pink rosebuds

1 pinback

Wire cutter

Glue suitable for metal

Glue gun/glue sticks

STEP 1

Prepare charm (see page 34).

STEP 2

Prepare a thick, 3-inch tassel with the variegated metallic colors of thread (see page 29). To prepare a wispy bow of gold, copper and silver metallic threads, tie thread ends together in a knot. Holding thread ends against the index card, wind thread around card to desired thickness. Do not cut thread. Carefully slip thread off card. Secure in center with craft wire to form a bow. Trim ends and fan threads. Set tassel and bow aside.

STEP 3

Tie a single bow of French wired ribbon, approximately 4 inches wide overall with 2 streamers (see page 27). Trim streamer ends to an inverted "V" shape.

STEP 4

Place tassel below French wired ribbon bow. Attach with a twist of wire. Glue wispy bow to center of wired ribbon bow.

STEP 5

With glue for metal, attach cherub-shaped charm to center of wired ribbon bow. Cherub-shaped charm will have threads of gold, copper and silver fanning out behind its wings.

STEP 6

With hot glue, attach rose-buds to top of tassel, overlapping onto bow and cherub-shaped charm. More rosebuds may be added to fill any gaps. With hot glue, attach pinback to back of wired ribbon bow.

BURGUNDY VALENTINE PIN

MATERIALS:

1 jewelry finding, stickpin

Small piece poster board

Red acrylic paint

1½ yards of ¼-inch-wide burgundy antique silk ribbon

Burgundy thread and needle

¼ yard of ⅛-inch-wide beige antique silk ribbon

One ¼-inch small pearl heart button

1 tiny heart-shaped brass locket

1 small preserved rose

Glue suitable for metal

Glue gun/glue sticks

STEP 1

Transfer small heart-shaped pattern, illustration 29, to poster board. Cut out. Paint one side red and set aside to dry.

illustration 29

STEP 2

Sew a running stitch with burgundy thread up middle of burgundy antique silk ribbon (see illustration 30). Pull thread to gather into ribbon ruffle. Tie knot in thread.

illustration 30

STEP 3

With hot glue, attach ribbon ruffle to poster board heart, following shape of heart. With hot glue, attach button to center of ribbon ruffle heart.

STEP 4

Tie a small 4-loop bow with beige silk ribbon (see page 27). Add two or more streamers, trimming to uneven lengths. With glue for metal, attach locket to longest streamer. With hot glue, attach bow to lower left side of ribbon ruffle heart.

STEP 5

With hot glue, attach rose just above bow, on side of ribbon ruffle heart.

STEP 6

Bend top portion of brass stickpin slightly. Starting at the top and pressing down, press stickpin through heart. With hot glue, secure stickpin to ribbon.

TIME TOGETHER

MATERIALS:

1 heart-shaped brass charm

1 birds on apple blossom branch-shaped brass charm

¼ yard of ½-inch-wide gold mesh French wired ribbon

Blue acrylic paint

Purple, green, and gold variegated silk or rayon thread

One 2-inch spike dried lavender

3 dried red rosebuds

1 pinback

Glue suitable for metal

Glue gun/glue sticks

STEP 1
Prepare charms
(see page 34).

STEP 2
Make single bow of gold mesh French wired ribbon approximately 3 inches wide overall, with streamers (see page 27).

STEP 3
With hot glue, attach lavender spike across center of wired ribbon bow, flower head on one side.

STEP 4
With glue for metal, secure heart-shaped charm to center of bow. With hot glue, attach rosebuds just below heart-shaped charm.

STEP 5
With glue for metal, attach streamers to underside of bird-shaped charm. The bird-shaped charm will act as a spacer.

STEP 6
With hot glue, attach pinback to back of wired ribbon bow.

ROSE COTTAGE

MATERIALS:

½ yard of 1½-inch-wide burgundy organdy ribbon

½ yard of 1-inch-wide pink to white French wired ombré ribbon

1 cherub-shaped brass charm

One 1-inch floral-embossed heart-shaped brass charm

5 red rosebuds

Several small sprigs preserved baby's breath

Gold craft wire

Gold, purple, variegated reds, variegated greens and blues silk or rayon thread for tassel

1 pinback

Wire cutter

Glue suitable for metal

Glue gun/glue sticks

STEP 1

Make one double bow of organdy ribbon, 3 inches wide overall, no streamers (see page 27). Secure center of organdy ribbon bow with a twist of wire. Set aside. Make triple bow of French wired ribbon, 2½ inches wide overall, no streamers (see page 27). Secure bow center with a twist of wire. Place ombré bow on top of organdy bow. Secure bows together with a twist of wire.

STEP 2

With glue for metal, attach cherub-shaped charm to center of bow. With glue for metal, attach heart-shaped charm to underside of cherub-shaped charm.

STEP 3

Make tassel with silk or rayon threads (see page 29). With glue for metal, attach top tassel wire to the underside of heart-shaped charm point.

STEP 4

With hot glue, attach 1 rosebud to center of heart-shaped charm. With hot glue, attach 4 rosebuds and baby's breath above cherub-shaped charm to form a crown. With hot glue, attach pinback into place.

FRIENDSHIP TUSSIE-MUSSIE

MATERIALS:

1 sheet heavy white paper for pattern

Four 4½-inch pieces florist's wire

Moss green florist's tape

Twenty-six 3-inch green silk leaves

Twenty 2-inch spikes of lavender

12 dried pink rosebuds

12 small sprigs dried thyme or rosemary

12 small dried white flowers

Few sprigs dried Queen Anne's lace

1 dried or freeze-dried pink rose

1½ yards of 1½-inch-wide iridescent dusty rose and spring green French wired ribbon

Scissors

Glue gun/glue sticks

STEP 1
Transfer tussie-mussie base pattern, illustration 31a, to white paper, (see page 34). Cut pattern out.

STEP 2
Glue silk leaves to top side of tussie-mussie base to form a ruff (see illustration 31b).

STEP 3
Holding four pieces of florist's wire together, wrap florist's tape around wire beginning at bottom. Leave ½ inch of wire unwrapped at top. Push unwrapped wire ends through center of tussie-mussie form. Bend over wired paper and leaf bases. With hot glue, secure wire to tussie-mussie form.

STEP 4
Glue lavender spikes in a sunburst pattern. Glue thyme or rosemary, white flowers and Queen Anne's lace in the spaces between the lavender spikes.

STEP 5
Glue small rosebuds over base of lavender spikes to form a nest, into which the pink rose is glued.

STEP 6
Finish tussie-mussie by tying a large 6-loop bow of French wired ribbon, 5 inches wide overall, with streamers (see page 27). Trim streamer ends in an inverted "V" shape. Glue bow to underside of tussie-mussie base.

illustration 31a

illustration 31b

EASTER

Spring pastels, starchy white lace, and the budding crocuses tell us winter has passed. The seasons change and the world looks fresh once again. Remember hunting for eggs in shiny new shoes? Recapture those times of joyful innocence while crafting these special Easter gifts.

These eggs are real shells, blown and adorned with scraps of paper and ribbon. Substitute artificial eggs for a gift that will be shipped. Why not decorate a keepsake egg for someone who made childhood such a treasured time?

VICTORIAN EASTER EGGS

mpty an eggshell intact by lightly tapping both ends of an egg with a needle until a small hole is formed at each end. Gently push needle through holes to break inner membranes. Rinse egg. Hold egg over bowl, place mouth over one hole and blow gently. Blow until all the yolk and white have been expelled from the shell. Hold egg under running water and allow some water to rinse out inside of shell. Blow water from eggshell and allow to dry.

VICTORIAN ROSE EGG

MATERIALS:

1 blown egg

Turquoise and gold acrylic paint

Round brush

Fan brush

1 Dresden silver paper snowflake

1 Dresden gold paper medallion

8 miniature silk roses in assorted colors

1 beige medallion rose with streamers

Scissors

White craft glue

STEP 1
With round brush, paint blown egg with turquoise paint. Allow paint to dry completely. Dip tip of fan brush in gold paint and streak blown egg lightly. Allow paint to dry completely.

STEP 2
Trim sections of Dresden snowflake to create silver caps for top and bottom of blown egg. Glue caps into place. Add elements of gold medallion as desired.

STEP 3
Glue silk roses on snowflake pieces as accents. Glue beige medallion rose with streamers on top of blown egg.

VICTORIAN COLLAGE EGG

MATERIALS:

1 blown egg

Soft blue and metallic gold acrylic paint

Round brush

Fan brush

Victorian paper scraps or Victorian wrapping paper

¾ yard of ⅛-inch-wide cream antique silk grosgrain ribbon

Scissors

White craft glue

STEP 1
With round brush, paint blown egg with soft blue paint. Allow paint to dry completely. Dip tips of fan brush in gold paint and streak blown egg lightly. Allow paint to dry completely. Set blown egg aside.

STEP 2
Cut out flowers, designs, and small portraits from paper scraps or wrapping paper. Glue a portrait scrap to blown egg as focal point, allowing other designs to overlap here and there.

STEP 3
Glue a piece of ribbon around blown egg, beginning and ending at top. Trim ends. Glue a second piece of ribbon around, crisscrossing with first piece of ribbon at bottom and creating four equal sections.

STEP 4
Use remaining ribbon to make a small, full bow with 4 streamers (see page 27). Glue bow to top of blown egg where ribbon ends meet. Twirl streamers down around blown egg, securing with dots of glue.

FIRST EASTER BASKET

MATERIALS:

1 small green basket with handle

5 yards of ⅝-inch-wide hand-painted rayon taffeta ribbon

17-20 open satin ribbon roses with green leaves

Glue gun/glue sticks

STEP 1
Measure handle of your Easter basket. Determine the number of yards of ribbon needed by referring to the Ladder Bow instructions (see page 27). Make ladder bows 3 inches wide overall to fit length of basket handle. Glue bow to basket handle.

STEP 2
Glue one rose to center of each bow.

EASTER BUNNY BOX

MATERIALS:

One 7-inch oval-shaped wooden box with lid

Cream, soft yellow, light moss green, moss green, light blue, white, gray, rose and medium pink acrylic paint

Natural sea sponge

Liner brush

Shader brush

¾ yard of ⅛-inch-wide bridal white Victorian scroll braid

¾ yard of ⅛-inch-wide pink rayon soutache

¾ yard of ⅜-inch-wide embroidered tape with ruffled edge

1 square white felt

White craft glue

STEP 1

Trace bottom of box onto felt. Cut out. Glue to box bottom.

STEP 2

With shader brush, paint interior of box with a color of your choice. Paint box top with white paint. Paint exterior edge of box top with yellow paint, and sides of box bottom with light moss green paint. Allow paint to dry before proceeding.

STEP 3

Using light blue paint, lightly sponge around outer 1½- to 2-inch edge of box. Allow paint to dry before proceeding.

STEP 4

Trace large bunny and rose wreath pattern, illustration 32. Transfer these patterns to center of box top (see page 34). Transfer small bunny and scattered roses pattern, illustration 33, around sides of box bottom, repeating transfer process as often as necessary to encircle box.

STEP 5

Using liner brush and gray paint, outline bunny on box top with fine gray line. Add details of pink ears, pink cheeks and a blue eye. Color in rose and heart details with rose and medium-pink paint (see photograph, page 53). Using light moss green and moss green paint, color stems and leaves. Use rose and moss green paints to add brushstroke details if desired.

STEP 6

Using liner brush, paint interior of wreath on box top around bunny with light blue paint, leaving an outline of white around roses and leaves. Paint heart with pink paint. Set box top aside to dry completely.

STEP 7

Paint bunnies on box bottom with white paint. Add details of pink ears, pink cheeks and a blue eye. Paint roses and leaves to match box top.

STEP 8

With craft glue, secure narrow soutache around box top at outside edge. Center ruffled tape around the sides of the box top. With craft glue, attach ruffled tape to box, allowing yellow paint to show above and below ruffled tape. With craft glue, attach Victorian scroll braid onto lower edge of box bottom.

illustration 32

illustration 33

MOTHER'S DAY

Chapters of life unfold... chubby fingers held tight for a first step... we graduate to ideas of our own... grow and begin to understand who this woman is— mother. She has given love and advice, given up dreams of her own so that we might have a chance to be all we can be. One day set aside to honor her never seems to be enough. On that day, we try to express our many thanks and loving feelings. This is the year to make a very special token of our love.

This multi-purpose bag can be used for potpourri, small gifts, or jewelry. Adapt this project for Christmas by substituting hunter green and burgundy ribbons.

WOVEN RIBBON SACHET

MATERIALS:

1⅓ yards violet French wired ribbon

2 yards of 1½-inch moss green French wired ribbon, set aside ¾ yard for tie

1¼ yards of ¾-inch hand-painted raspberry rayon taffeta ribbon

7x9-inch piece violet, raspberry or moss green silk or other soft fabric

Coordinating thread and needle

8½x11-inch piece cardboard

Masking tape

Round brush

Water

Fabric glue

Test glue on ribbon scrap to check for seepage.

STEP 1

Cut violet ribbon into four equal lengths of 12 inches. Cut moss green ribbon into six equal lengths of 7 inches. Cut raspberry ribbon into six equal lengths of 7 inches.

STEP 2

Brush small amount of glue onto raspberry ribbon. Mount raspberry ribbon on moss green ribbon to form a center stripe. Repeat with remaining raspberry and green ribbon pieces. Clean brush often.

STEP 3

Carefully lay the 4 pieces of violet ribbon side-by-side on cardboard. Make sure that ribbon edges touch but do not overlap.

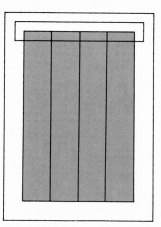

illustration 34

With tape, secure top of ribbon pieces, ½-inch down from top, to cardboard (see illustration 34).

HOW TO HANG YOUR WREATH

To add a hanger to your wreath, cut one 6-inch piece of florist's wire. Push one end through back of wreath base. Twist ends together to form a circle.

LE FOLLET

Boulevard St. Martin, 61.

STEP 4

Lift up the second and fourth violet ribbons. Lay moss green ribbon with raspberry ribbon stripe across the first and third ribbons (see illustration 35). Return the second and fourth ribbons to original flat position. Lift up the first and third ribbons. Lay 1 moss green ribbon with raspberry ribbon stripe across the second and fourth ribbons (illustration 36). Secure ribbons together with light touch of glue under top squares. Repeat this procedure for all four sections of green ribbon (see illustration 37). Allow glue to set before proceeding.

STEP 5

Carefully remove tape. Turn up one entire woven ribbon section at bottom edge of sachet. Turn down one entire woven ribbon section at top edge of sachet. Set aside.

STEP 6

Turn under ½ inch along all sides of fabric and press. Hand-stitch or glue to woven ribbon back. Finished size is approximately 6x8 inches.

STEP 7

Fill bag with potpourri or small gift. With ¾ yard of moss green ribbon, make a single bow around top of bag to close (see page 27).

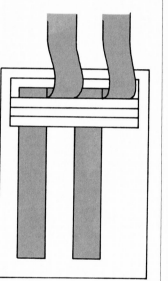

illustration 35

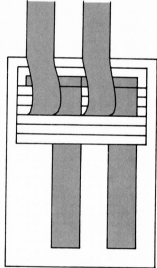

illustration 36

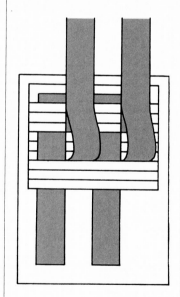

illustration 37

VICTORIAN CHARM PILLOW

MATERIALS:

The weaving ribbons are for the pillow shell. Substitute colors of ribbon that please you.

WEAVING RIBBONS:

⅔ yard each of:

1-inch-wide mauve French wired ribbon

⅝-inch-wide soft rose French wired ribbon

⅝-inch-wide celery green French wired ribbon

⅝-inch-wide gold-edge, gold floral stripe French wired ribbon

⅜-inch-wide cream French wired ribbon

⅝-inch-wide plum hand-painted rayon taffeta ribbon

⅝-inch-wide rose hand-painted rayon taffeta ribbon

⅝-inch-wide pale pink hand-painted rayon taffeta ribbon

⅝-inch-wide turquoise hand-painted rayon taffeta ribbon

¼-inch-wide blue hand-painted rayon taffeta ribbon

¼-inch-wide moss green hand-painted rayon taffeta ribbon

1-inch-wide striped, gold-edged ombré ribbon

1-inch-wide white-on-white brocade ribbon

FOR DECORATION:

¼ yard of ¼-inch-wide wine red antique silk ribbon

¼ yard of small metallic silver cord

¾ yard of ¼-inch-wide snow-white picot-edged braid

3 miniature open roses in coordinating colors

1 small satin rosebud with green leaves

1 shaded silk rose with leaves

1 small cream rosebud with bow

1 small preserved rosebud

1 filigree heart-shaped brass charm

1 antique-silver heart-shaped button

1 pewter heart button

1 round heart-patterned button

7x7-inch square fine-textured, soft fabric

1 handful dried lavender

Cotton batting

¾ yard of ¼-inch-wide snow-white picot-edged braid

Masking tape

One 8x10-inch piece cardboard

White fabric glue

Small watercolor brush

STEP 1
Cut ribbon for weaving into three 8-inch lengths.

STEP 2
On cardboard, place mixed colors and widths to achieve an overall width of 6 inches. Tape into place with masking tape, ½ inch down from tops of ribbon ends (see illustration 34, page 56). Make sure ribbon edges touch but do not overlap.

STEP 3
Mixing colors and widths, weave remaining ribbons until a length of 6 inches is reached (see illustrations 35, 36, and 37, page 58). Secure ribbons together with light touch of fabric glue under top squares. Allow glue to dry before proceeding.

STEP 4
Carefully remove tape. Trim away excess ribbon ends, leaving ¼ to ½ inch. Turn all ribbon ends toward underside of square and glue into place. Set pillow front aside.

STEP 5
Iron under ½ inch seam allowance on all sides of 7x7-inch square of soft fabric.

STEP 6
Using a slip stitch, sew three sides of ribbon square to fabric (see illustration 38). Fill with lavender and batting and stitch closed.

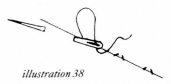

illustration 38

STEP 7
Glue picot-edged trim to front edges of pillow on all four sides. Decorate pillow with buttons, charms, trims and ribbon scraps.

Thoughts of Mother in the month of May fill the heart with love. As we tend the spring garden, much as Mother cared for us when we were young, we cannot help reflecting on her love and devotion.

MOTHER'S DAY WREATH

MATERIALS:

One 10-inch round straw wreath

2 small dried Madonna lilies

4 dried blue delphinium blossoms

6 dried bachelor's buttons

7 dried pansies

10 dried pink roses

Mix of dried sweet William, yarrow, nigella, chrysanthemum, cosmos, rosebuds, geum, ferns, Queen Anne's lace, daisies

20 to 30 dried green leaves

1¼ yards of ¾-inch-wide blue hand-painted rayon taffeta ribbon

French lilac or tuberose essential oil (optional)

Glue gun/glue sticks

ssemble flowers on a tray or paper before making the wreath. With the exception of the dried pink roses, the flowers listed above were grown and collected from my garden. Substitute purchased leaves and flowers as necessary.

Scent your Mother's Day wreath by rubbing a few drops of essential oil onto the back of the straw wreath before adding the flowers.

For better durability in shipping wreaths, treat flowers with a preservative (see page 12).

STEP 1

Working in small sections, cover front and sides of wreath with hot glue, adding flowers as you go. Distribute main flowers evenly, filling in with smaller blossoms.

STEP 2

With the rayon taffeta ribbon, make a 6-loop bow, 3 inches wide overall, with double streamers (see page 27). Glue bow to center of wreath.

SILK SURPRISE BOX

MATERIALS:

One 1¾-inch diameter round wooden box with top

One 1¾-inch diameter poster board circle

1 liner brush

Variegated greens and blues, gold, metallic emerald, violet, bright blue, and deep purple silk or rayon thread

¼ yard of ½-inch-wide antique gold metallic gimp

¼ yard of ⅛-inch-wide antique gold metallic soutache

1 medium-size filigree or antique gold bead

One 1¾-inch diameter piece felt, coordinating color

White craft glue

Glue gun/glue sticks

STEP 1

Unwind thread ends from spools. Knot these ends together. With hot glue, secure knot to center of poster board circle.

STEP 2

Holding threads together, wind around and around circle, crossing threads at center to create many layers of color radiating from circle center. (If threads tend to slip out of place as you work, simply rub a dot of craft glue on them to secure.) With hot glue, attach poster board circle to box top. Center of circle will be thicker than sides, but metallic soutache will compensate.

STEP 3

With hot glue, attach metallic gimp to encircle sides of box top.

STEP 4

Glue metallic soutache around rim of box top above braid. This trim will overlap threaded circle for a finished look.

STEP 5

Place lid on box. Carefully apply thin coat of craft glue to section below lid, making sure glue does not touch braid. Wind threads around glued section until a layer of thread covers area completely, usually 6 or 7 threads deep will suffice. Secure thread ends with craft glue.

STEP 6

Glue gold bead to center of box top. Glue felt to box bottom to finish.

Victorian lace and lavender, all tied with delicate ribbons, make a gift Mother will long remember.

SACHET FOR MOTHER

MATERIALS:

1 yard of ⅝-inch-wide iridescent yellow with pink border French wired ribbon

1 yard of ¼-inch-wide dusty peach antique silk ribbon

1 miniature preserved rose

One 4x9-inch piece lace with a scalloped edge

1 "Mother" brass charm

1 triple silk rosette

½ ounce dried lavender

Glue suitable for metal

Glue gun/glue sticks

STEP 1

Fold 4-inch sides of lace to form back seam. Glue or stitch together to secure. Glue or stitch bottom edges together to form a bag. Finished sachet measures approximately 4x4½ inches.

STEP 2

Fill lace sachet with dried lavender. Pinch lace together at top of bag. Place a dot of hot glue in gathered center to close bag. Hold gathered lace closed until glue sets.

STEP 3

Set aside an 8-inch piece of French wired ribbon. Make a 6-loop bow, approximately 3 inches wide overall, with four streamers (see page 27). Trim streamer ends in an inverted "V" shape.

STEP 4

Using antique silk ribbon, make a small 6-loop bow, approximately 2 inches wide overall, with six streamers (see page 27).

STEP 5

Glue wired ribbon bow to top of sachet. Attach peach bow to center, allowing streamers to fall on front section of sachet. Glue rose to center of peach bow.

STEP 6

With glue for metal, attach "Mother" charm to sachet. With hot glue, attach triple silk rosette to sachet just below charm.

It is possible
to "paint" paper
and notecards with
essential oils directly.
It leaves a barely
distinguishable pattern
on the paper, and a
wonderful scent that
lasts for a long time!
Scent stationery and
greeting cards, store
them in a closed con-
tainer with lavender
or potpourri for
two weeks.

GIFTS FOR SPRING

The gift of a quiet walk in the spring woods...returning with a bouquet of flowers to press and give. Perhaps this is the day to take a few moments to collect violets and thank a friend.

Personalize a gift with the signature of scent, and decorate your ink bottle with a hand-colored label. Make a photocopy of this label, color the border with water-color, and glue on a small pressed flower.

LAVENDER-SCENTED INK

Permission granted to photocopy this label for personal use only.

MATERIALS:

¼ cup dried lavender

Boiling water to cover

Strainer

Bowl

Bottle of ink

STEP 1

Place dried lavender in bowl. Pour enough boiling water over lavender to cover. Let cool and strain, discarding blossoms.

STEP 2

Add approximately one teaspoon of scented water to ink.

PRESSED VIOLET STATIONERY FOLDER

MATERIALS:

One 11x12-inch sheet of handmade French paper with flowers

Selection of pressed violets, leaves, and ferns

3-5 spikes dried lavender

1¼ yards of iridescent purple and green French wired ribbon

Liner brush

Small double boiler

Lavender-scented votive candle

Ruler

Scissors

White craft glue

STEP 1
Fold bottom edge of paper up 2 inches (see illustration 39). Secure sides of 2-inch fold with glue. Create folder by folding paper in half.

STEP 2
With brush, apply craft glue to back of violets, ferns, and leaves. Press into place on front of folder. Allow glue to set completely.

STEP 3
Melt scented votive candle in doubleboiler. With brush, apply a thin coat of melted wax over violets, ferns, and leaves to protect and scent them (see page 16). (Brush needs to be cleaned in very hot water.)

STEP 4
Place desired stationery or cards in folder. Tie with ribbon and spikes of lavender.

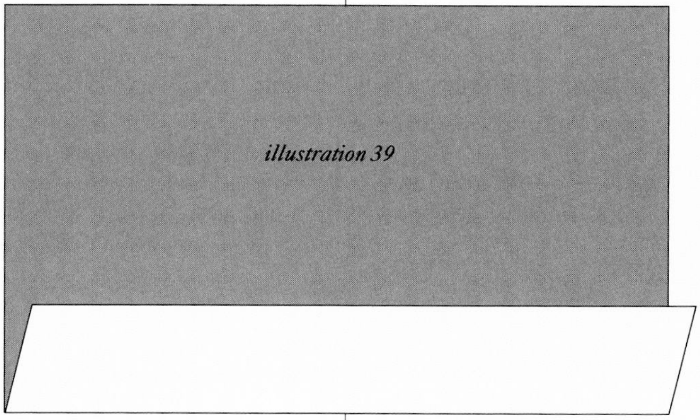

illustration 39

The lavender plant is the most wonderful combination of soft green and purple hues. The silk fabric used here provides an iridescent complement to the scent it holds.

LAVENDER DESK SACHET

MATERIALS:

Two 5½x10-inch pieces of gold and purple iridescent silk or other sheer fabric

½ yard of ⅝-inch-wide hunter green French wired ribbon

1½ ounces dried lavender

Pinking or scalloping shears

Glue gun/glue sticks

STEP 1

Place rectangles right sides together. Glue long sides and one short side together. Let glue dry completely. Turn right side out.

STEP 2

With shears, trim edges of open side of sachet. Fill bag with lavender. Gather top edge of sachet. Tie sachet closed with simple, single bow of wired ribbon (see page 27).

DELIGHT
REIGNS
IN A
GARDEN

WELCOME GIFTS

Welcome to a new neighbor, good wishes to warm a new home...the gift of a flowering plant is always gratefully received. Flowers are further enhanced when the crafter adds a personal touch to a simple clay pot found or purchased for the occasion.

Paint clay pots, sponging and ragging for special effects. Decorated pots are especially suited to herbal topiaries or dried arrangements. Adapt this project for use as wedding table centerpieces by substituting cream and white paint and white French wired ribbons.

IVY AND BERRIES

MATERIALS:

One 5-inch clay bulb pot

Lavender blue and violet acrylic paint

Shader brush

Fan brush

Two 4-inch stems paper ivy leaves

One 4-inch stem white and raspberry berries

Wire cutter

Glue gun/glue sticks

STEP 1
With shader brush, paint flowerpot exterior and 3-inch depth of interior of pot with lavender blue paint. Allow paint to dry before proceeding.

STEP 2
Streak pot lightly with dry fan brush dipped in small amount of violet paint. Allow paint to dry before proceeding.

STEP 3
Twist ivy to form a pleasing shape over front of pot. Glue ivy stem into place. Glue berry stem among the ivy.

HEATHER GARLAND

MATERIALS:

One 6-inch standard flowerpot

Pale aqua and pale lavender blue acrylic paint

Shader brush

Natural sea sponge

2 stems white and heather pink paper wildflower sprays

1½ yards of ½-inch-wide green shaded to lilac French wired ombré ribbon

Wire cutter

Glue gun/glue sticks

STEP 1

With shader brush, paint flowerpot exterior and 3-inch depth of pot interior with pale aqua paint. Allow paint to dry before proceeding.

STEP 2

Lightly sponge a pattern of lavender blue paint on pot (see page 32). Allow paint to dry before proceeding.

STEP 3

Encircle pot with ribbon just below rim. Cut to size. Glue ribbon into place. Use remaining ribbon for bow in Step 5.

STEP 4

Separate paper flowers into six sprigs. Set aside sprigs and any remaining flowers. Alternating pink and white sprigs, glue sprigs to ribbon, forming a garland.

STEP 5

With remaining ribbon, make a 6-loop bow, approximately 4 inches wide overall with two streamers (see page 27). Finish streamer ends in an inverted "V" shape. Glue bow to center of garland. Glue any remaining sprigs around the bow.

FRUITS OF SUMMER

MATERIALS:

One 7-inch clay urn

Pale moss green, light aqua green, and medium blue violet acrylic paint

Shader brush

Natural sea sponge

1 yard of ⅝-inch-wide hyacinth blue hand-painted rayon taffeta ribbon

1 spray red grapes, shaded with green

1 small spray black grapes with leaves

Glue gun/glue sticks

STEP 1
With shader brush, paint lip of flowerpot and a 3-inch depth of interior with light moss green paint. Allow paint to dry before proceeding.

STEP 2
Paint remaining pot exterior with light aqua green paint. Allow paint to dry before proceeding.

STEP 3
Using blue violet paint, lightly sponge a pattern (see page 32). Allow paint to dry before proceeding.

STEP 4
Encircle pot with ribbon approximately 1 inch below lip. Cut to size.

STEP 5
Use remaining ribbon to make a 6-loop bow , 3 inches wide overall, with two streamers (see page 27). Trim streamer ends to an inverted "V" shape. Glue bow to center of ribbon band.

STEP 6
Arrange fruit clusters behind bow loops and glue into place.

WEDDING GIFTS

An invitation to join the celebration of a beginning. Hope and love fill the day as we gather with wishes for a bright future. We feel warmed and reminded of the days that mark our lives. Gifts most cherished are those received on our wedding day.

JUNE ROSES

MATERIALS:

1 basket with handle (approximately 8x5x4-inch)

White, moss green, and metallic gold acrylic paint

Shader brush

1 block florist's oasis

Green sphagnum moss

2 yards of 1½-inch-wide cream organdy ribbon

12 freeze-dried white rose

Glue gun/glue sticks

STEP 1
Spray entire basket with warm water to saturate before painting. This allows the basket to accept paint easily, and paint will feed into the crevices readily.

STEP 2
Paint basket body with white paint. Allow paint to dry before proceeding. Paint basket rim and handle with green paint. Allow paint to dry before proceeding.

STEP 3
With tips of brush dipped in small amount of gold paint, streak basket lightly to accent. Allow paint to dry before proceeding.

STEP 4
Cut oasis (see illustration 40). With hot glue, secure oasis in basket.

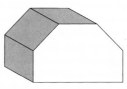

illustration 40

STEP 5
Glue moss onto oasis to cover completely. Glue roses directly to moss, spacing evenly.

STEP 6
Make a 6-loop bow, 5 inches wide overall, with extra streamers (see page 27). Glue to handle.

WEDDING DIARY

MATERIALS:

One 6x8½-inch blank book

One 10x17-inch piece bridal white raw silk cut with pinking shears

Cotton batting cut to fit around book exterior

One 10x13-inch piece antique lace cut with pinking shears

1 yard of ½-inch-wide antique lace trim

1 off-white silk medallion rose with streamers

Fabric glue

Glue gun/glue sticks

STEP 1

Place raw silk on flat surface, right side up. Position antique lace rectangle over raw silk so that left-hand sides align. Four inches of raw silk on right-hand side will remain exposed. Working in sections, lift edge of lace and apply a ½-inch band of fabric glue to raw silk. To secure, gently smooth lace back into place. Allow glue to dry completely.

STEP 2

Turn lace and raw silk rectangle right side down. Center cotton batting on fabric. A 1-inch margin of fabric will be exposed along top and bottom edge. A 2-inch margin of fabric will be exposed on each side. Working in sections, lift edge of batting and apply a ½-inch band of fabric glue to silk. To secure, gently smooth back into place.

STEP 3

Fold fabric into place over batting (see illustration 41). With fabric glue, secure fabric to batting. To create book cover pockets, fold remaining 2-inch margins of silk over batting (see illustration 41). With a thin line of hot glue at outermost edge, attach silk edges together. Be sure to keep glue at extreme outer edge so cover will fit book.

STEP 4

Slip book into cover.

STEP 5

Using antique lace trim, make a double bow, 2 inches wide overall, with two streamers (see page 27). Using hot glue, attach to upper left corner of cover. Using hot glue, attach medallion rose with streamers to center of lace bow.

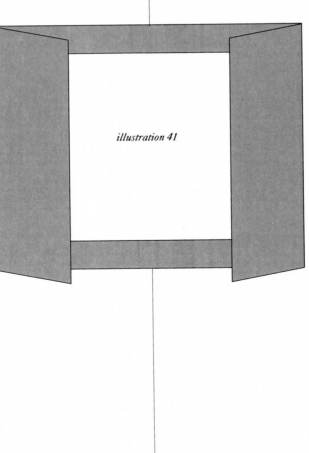

illustration 41

GIFT OF BLESSINGS

 ecorate this little wedding box and fill it with thoughtful blessings for the happy couple. Photocopy these blessings. Add messages of your own, color motifs, and cut out strips to fill a box or perhaps a lovely bowl.

MATERIALS:

One 3x1½-inch round wooden box with lid

One 10x10-inch piece bridal white raw silk

Cotton batting

12 inches of ½-inch-wide lace trim with pearls

12 inches pearl trim

12 inches of ½-inch-wide delicate lace

1½ yards of ½-inch-wide gold floral stripe French wired ribbon

Round brush

Gold metallic acrylic paint

Pale color fine-tipped fabric marker

Pencil

1 square white felt

Fabric glue

Glue gun/glue sticks

STEP 1
Paint interior of box with gold paint. Allow paint to dry before proceeding.

STEP 2
Place lid on wrong side of raw silk. Trace lid, using fabric marker. Cut out, allowing ½ inch all around marking. Set aside. Place box bottom on white felt, trace bottom. Cut out. Glue into place.

STEP 3
Cut an exact circle of cotton batting to fit top of box. Glue into place. Place silk piece on batting right side up. With fabric glue, secure edges of silk to sides of lid.

STEP 4
Glue delicate lace around edge of box top. Glue pearl trim around bottom edge of lace.

STEP 5
Using gold floral French wired ribbon, make a chain of single knots, allowing ¼ inch between each knot. Trim ends. With hot glue, secure ribbon knot chain around top of lid.

STEP 6
With gold floral French wired ribbon, make a small 8-loop bow, 2 inches wide overall (see page 27). Glue to center of box top.

STEP 7
Place lid on box. With pencil, draw lightly around bottom edge of lid. Remove lid. Cut strip of raw silk same width as box from pencil line to bottom edge. Encircle box with strip of silk. Cut to size. With fabric glue, glue into place. Glue lace and pearl trim around bottom edge of box.

WEDDING BLESSINGS

Permission granted to photocopy this page for personal use only. Create your own blessings as well.

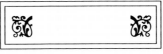

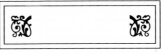

ANNIVERSARY GIFTS

Silver and golden memories of all the holidays spent together as a family...we gather once again, reunited in celebration of a long life together. Craft a tribute in recognition of your family's constant devotion throughout the years.

The gardenia can hardly be improved upon, but the elegance of gilding this freeze-dried bloom creates a feeling of timelessness. To add fragrance, simply add a few drops of gardenia oil to leaf edges with a bit of cotton.

KEEPSAKE GARDENIA

MATERIALS:

1 freeze-dried gardenia with leaves

Deep metallic gold acrylic paint

Round brush

Water

Plate for mixing paint

Mix a wash of water and a small amount of gold paint (see page 33). With round brush, gently paint gardenia, petal by petal. Paint leaves if desired. Allow paint to dry completely. This will create a mottled glaze of gold.

Little souvenirs of a lifetime together surely need a special nesting place. This small silver box, for cherished trinkets, is simple enough for the grandchildren to make.

SILVER ANNIVERSARY BOX

MATERIALS:

One 4½x3½x2-inch oval wooden box with lid

Metallic silver acrylic paint

Round brush

3 Dresden silver paper snowflakes

¾ yard of ¼-inch-wide silver metallic grosgrain ribbon

½ yard of ¼-inch-wide silver metallic rickrack

¾ yard of ¼-inch-wide soft gray single-edged picot trim

1 mesh bow brass charm

Scissors

Glue suitable for metal

Glue gun/glue sticks

STEP 1

Paint all box surfaces with silver paint. Allow paint to dry before proceeding. Prepare charm for painting (see page 34). Paint charm with silver paint. Set aside.

STEP 2

Encircle the box with grosgrain ribbon. Cut to size. Cut 2 more pieces the same size. Set one piece aside. With hot glue, glue 2 pieces of grosgrain ribbon around edge of box top. Center and glue rickrack around box top side. Glue picot trim around box top edge. Loops of picot will overlap onto surface of box top.

STEP 3

Glue one snowflake to center of box top. With glue for metal, attach charm to snowflake center. Set aside.

STEP 4

Cut remaining paper snowflakes in half. Align straight edge of a snowflake with bottom edge of box. With hot glue, attach snowflake to box. Using remaining grosgrain ribbon, glue ribbon to cover bottom edges of snowflakes. Glue remaining picot trim to top edge of ribbon.

GOLDEN ANNIVERSARY MEMORIES

MATERIALS:

Precut double mat to fit photograph

1 sheet metallic gold tissue paper

Acid-free mat board

Acid-free tape

1 yard of ¼-inch-wide gold metallic cord

1¼ yards of ⅛-inch-wide gold and green metallic cord

Iron

Craft knife

White craft glue

Glue gun/glue sticks

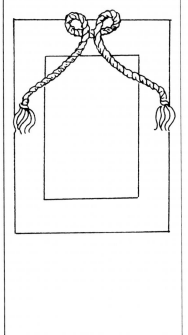

STEP 1
Crumple tissue paper, forming a ball. Carefully open and flatten without smoothing out wrinkles. Heat iron to lowest setting. Press wrinkles into tissue paper. Be sure to work quickly so the iron has only brief contact with the paper.

STEP 2
Separate double mat from mat backing. Set backing aside. Separate inner liner mat from outer frame mat. Set inner mat aside. Spread a thin coat of craft glue over the entire face of the top mat (including edges). Place mat face down on the wrong side of tissue paper and press firmly. Trim tissue paper around outer edges leaving 1½-inch border.

STEP 3
Cut out center of tissue paper, leaving 1-inch border around the inside of mat. Slit tissue paper diagonally at corners. Turn mat face down. Spread a thin 1½-inch band of craft glue on back of mat around edges. Wrap tissue paper around mat edges and smooth onto glued areas. Center inner mat on wrong side of tissue-covered mat. Using hot glue, secure mats together.

fold here

illustration 42

STEP 4
Position photograph on mat board, lining it up carefully with the openings of the mats. Using acid-free tape, secure photograph corners into place. With hot glue, secure mats together.

STEP 5
With hot glue, attach narrow cord to outside edge of frame. Glue center point of cord to top center of frame. Loop cord around on each side and glue into place. Tie off ends to form tassels and glue into place.

STEP 6
Transfer triangle pattern, illustration 42, to mat board (see page 34). Cut out. Position and glue tab to frame back as stand.

To ensure
your child's safety,
use fabric paints
with glitter mixed in
for clothing items.
Hand washing is the
safest way to clean
painted fabric. If you
machine-wash, put
item in a pillow case,
close and wash
on the delicate cycle in
cool water. Hang to
dry. Ironing is not
recommended.

GIFTS FOR BABY

Happiest of all is the day of Baby's arrival. It is a time for great celebration and gifts. Making presents for the baby is such a delightful endeavor. We fashion delicate colors and tiny rosebuds for the little one, and cherish this time of perfect innocence.

SWEETHEART PHOTO FRAME

MATERIALS:

Three 6x6-inch squares poster board

One 6x6-inch square cotton batting

One 6x6-inch square white cotton fabric

One 5-inch square Battenberg lace doily

1 each of pink, white and blue silk ribbon roses with leaves

3 silk rosette bands with center rose

1 triple beaded ribbon flower with leaves

Scissors

Glue gun/glue sticks

STEP 1

Transfer triangle pattern, (see illustration 42, page 79) to poster board square (see page 34). Cut out and fold on dotted line. Set aside. Transfer heart-shaped pattern, illustration 43, to two poster board squares. Cut out, and set one heart aside. Cut out center from remaining heart. Cut one batting heart to fit heart shape exactly and set aside.

illustration 43

cut out one heart shape

STEP 2

Place white cotton fabric, right side down, on flat surface. Position heart on fabric. Draw around shape, adding a ½ inch allowance. Mark slit lines, illustration 44, on allowance. Cut out heart shape and slit fabric. Set fabric heart aside.

STEP 3

Glue batting heart to poster board shape. Position heart, batting side down, on wrong side of fabric heart. With hot glue, work in small sections and glue fabric edges around heart form, pulling fabric gently. Glue outside edges first. Set aside.

STEP 4

Trim one corner from Battenberg lace square and position three corners of lace on back of remaining heart-shaped poster board. Lace points will be facing upward and to each side. White side of poster board will be facing outward. Heart will act as backing for doily. Glue lace to poster board.

STEP 5

Lay doily-covered heart, doily facing upward, on flat surface. Glue padded heart and doily heart to form a partial pocket. Begin at bottom and continue gluing about 2 inches up on each side. Be sure to keep glue toward outermost edge.

STEP 6

Glue silk rosette bands around heart. Glue single silk rosettes at top and sides near frame. Glue cluster of roses at heart indentation.

STEP 7

Position triangle tab on back of frame to create a stand. Glue into place. Let glue dry completely.

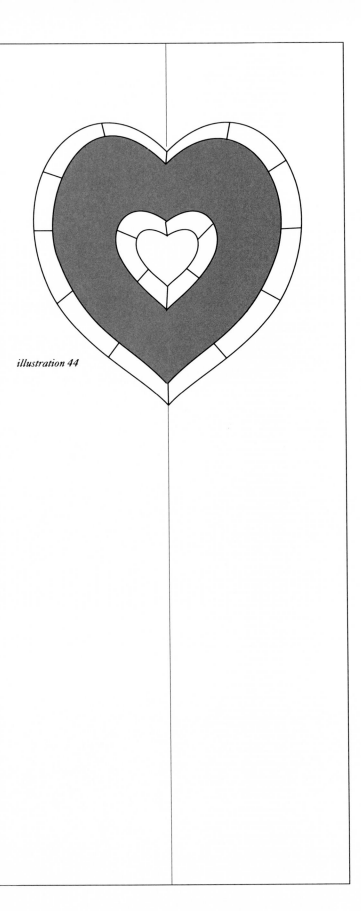

illustration 44

TEDDY BEAR SHIRT

MATERIALS:

1 infant T-shirt

Light green, light blue, medium blue, light yellow-orange, tan, and medium pink acrylic paint

Glittering blue, glittering yellow, iridescent brown and glossy black squeeze-bottle fabric paint

Round brush

Liner brush

6 small white heart buttons

One 1-inch blue bow button

1 small blue-and-white heart button

1 small light yellow satin rosebud with green leaves

5 inches of ¼-inch-wide medium blue double-sided satin ribbon

Blue thread and needle

Light blue iron-on transfer pen

STEP 1

Prepare garment for painting (see page 33). Using light blue iron-on transfer pen, transfer pattern, illustration 45, to shirt front just below neckline (see page 80).

STEP 2

Use acrylic paints for the following details. With round brush, paint teddy bear with tan paint. Paint horse with light blue paint, leaving hearts white. Paint mane and tail with medium blue paint. Paint saddle with light yellow-orange paint. Paint rocker with light green paint. Allow paint to dry before proceeding. Use liner brush to paint teddy bear's ears, mouth and cheeks with medium pink paint.

STEP 3

Use squeeze-bottle paint for the following details. Add eyes and nose for teddy bear, and paint eye for horse with black paint. Outline teddy bear with iridescent brown. Outline horse and saddle with glittering yellow paint. Outline mane and tail with glittering blue paint. Outline rocker with glittering blue paint with yellow dots added to top edge. Allow paint to dry before proceeding.

STEP 4

Sew white heart buttons on selected rocking-horse hearts. Sew blue bow button to rocking horse's neck for a bow tie. Sew yellow rosebud to teddy bear's right shoulder.

STEP 5

Make small single bow of blue satin ribbon (see page 27). Sew bow to shirt at center of neckline. Sew blue-and-white heart button to center of bow.

illustration 45

BUNNY'S GARDEN

MATERIALS:

1 infant T-shirt

Light green, light brown, light orange, light rose, and medium rose acrylic paint

Iridescent beige, iridescent green, light pink, and blue squeeze-bottle fabric paint

Round brush

Liner brush

2 miniature pink open silk roses

2 miniature apricot open silk roses

1 palest pink open satin rose with green leaves

1 small lace heart with satin-rose center

2 small embroidered flower-trim bouquets of mixed colors

⅓ yard of embroidered pink-and-green tape with ruffled white edge

2 to 3 tiny baby dress buttons

2 tiny baby pearl buttons

White and pink thread and needle

Pink iron-on transfer pen

STEP 1

Prepare garment for painting (see page 33). Using pink iron-on transfer pen, transfer illustration 46 to shirt front just below neckline (see photograph, page 80).

STEP 2

Use acrylic paints for the following details. With round brush, paint dress with light rose paint and ear markings, heart cheeks, and shoes with medium rose paint. Paint basket with light brown paint, carrots with light orange paint, carrot tops, flower stems, and stocking stripes with light green paint. Allow paint to dry before proceeding.

STEP 3

Use squeeze-bottle paints for the following details. Outline dress with light pink paint. Draw nose and mouth with light pink paint. Outline head, hands and feet with iridescent beige paint. Outline carrot tops, and carrot detail with iridescent green paint. Allow paint to dry before proceeding.

STEP 4

Using pink thread, sew baby dress buttons on bunny's dress. Sew pearl buttons on shoes. Sew miniature open roses to top of painted flower stems, alternating colors. Sew embroidered trim bouquets to bunny's basket. Sew lace heart to create a jabot (ruffled collar).

STEP 5

Fold end of tape under ¼ inch and sew around neckline from shoulder seam to shoulder seam. With white thread, stitch tape around neckline front, approximately ⅜ inch from neckline edge. Sew large, open rose to ribbon tape at center of neckline.

illustration 46

GIFTS FOR CHILDREN

Sunny childhood days are made more lovely by getting lots of presents!
Sometimes the greatest reason for giving a gift is simply for love.
We craft today the heirlooms of tomorrow, made with a caring hand
for them to give, one day, to children of their own.

Frame a little print or photograph in this small flower-box window frame. Someone small will appreciate a view of his or her own.

PLAYHOUSE WINDOW

MATERIALS:

One 9½ x 8-inch unpainted wooden window frame

Cobalt blue, cream, and light apple green acrylic paint

¼ yard of ¾-inch-wide pink French wired ribbon

Silk flowers to fill window box

1 greeting card or print to fit window

Picture hanger

Glue gun/glue sticks

STEP 1
Paint inner window frame sections with cream paint, outside of frame with blue paint, and window box with green paint. Allow paint to dry before proceeding.

STEP 2
Make a single bow of French wired ribbon (see page 27). Glue bow to top of window frame.

STEP 3
Position print behind window frame. Secure in place with glue. Trim edges. Glue or fasten hanger into place. Place flowers in window box.

MATERIALS FOR DOLL:

½ yard of fine-textured muslin

Pink thread and needle

Cotton batting

2 tiny round black buttons

Handful of curly doll hair

Scissors

MATERIALS FOR DRESS:

¼ yard of floral print cotton fabric

9x4-inch piece coordinated fabric for collar

⅔ yard of 2-inch-wide Battenberg lace

Nonwoven interfacing

⅓ yard of ⅛-inch-wide pink antique silk ribbon

1 small pink satin rosebud

Silk ribbon rose tape

Pins

Scissors

TO MAKE DOLL:
STEP 1
Enlarge pattern, illustration 47, to full size (see page 34). Transfer pattern to fabric (see page 34). Cut out 2 body shapes. Pin right sides together and machine-stitch, leaving bottom of body shapes open.

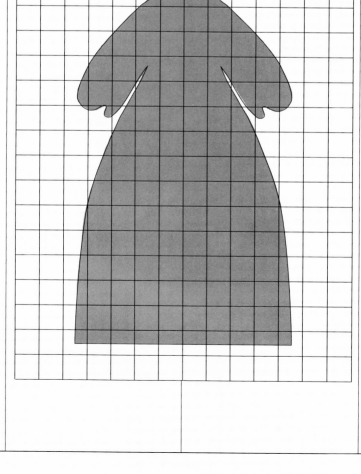

illustration 47
1 square = 1 inch

STEP 2
Turn body shape right side out. Stuff with batting to desired firmness. Slip-stitch opening closed (see illustration 48).

Sew on button eyes. With pink thread, form the nose with a French knot (see illustration 49), and use a chain stitch to form the smiling mouth (see illustration 50). Arrange and glue the doll's hair.

illustration 48

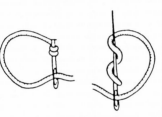

illustration 49

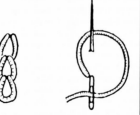

illustration 50

TO MAKE DRESS:

STEP 1

Enlarge dress pattern, illustration 51, to full size (see page 34). Transfer dress pattern to wrong side of folded fabric, positioning shoulders along fold (see page 34). Cut out. Enlarge collar pattern, illustration 51, to full size (see page 34). Transfer collar pattern to fabric and interfacing. Cut out 2 collar pieces from fabric and 1 piece from interfacing.

STEP 2

Align collar pieces, right sides together. Place interface piece on top of collar pieces. Pin all three pieces together. Sew along outer edge of collar. Leave neckline curve open for turning. Turn collar right side out and press. Stitch open end closed.

STEP 3

Lay dress body flat, wrong side up, and pin collar into place. Stitch along neck opening, following inside edge of collar. Turn collar through neck opening and press.

STEP 4

Fold dress at shoulders so that right sides are together. Stitch along side seams.

STEP 5

Hem bottom of dress.

STEP 6

Cut out one 2-inch section of lace. Tack lace under collar for decoration. Make a small single bow of antique lace (see page 27). Attach bow to center of collar. Sew rosebud to center of bow. Sew remaining lace around bottom of dress. Place garland of ribbon rose tape on doll's head.

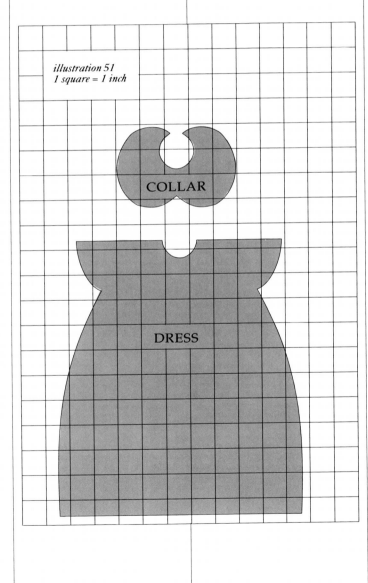

illustration 51
1 square = 1 inch

COLLAR

DRESS

KITTY FRIEND

MATERIALS:

½ yard of white-on-white chintz fabric

½ yard of 1-inch-wide pale green French wired ribbon

Dusty rose, pink, light blue, medium blue, and black acrylic paint

Cotton batting

Liner brush

White thread and needle

Scissors

Iron

STEP 1

Enlarge pattern, illustrations 52a and 52b, to full size (see page 34). Transfer patterns to wrong side of fabric (see page 34). Cut out 2 body shapes and 1 bottom oval. Turn over 1 body shape and transfer face and details to right side of fabric (see page 34).

STEP 2

Place kitty's body shapes right sides together. Sew together. Sew bottom oval to body, leaving 2 or 3 inches open for stuffing. Turn right sides out and press.

STEP 3

Fill with cotton batting to desired firmness. Using slip stitch, close bottom (see illustration 53).

illustration 53

STEP 4

Paint body details with rose paint and interior of ears and heart with pink paint. Paint eyes with blue paint and paint outline and centers with black paint. Add light blue dots around heart. Allow paint to dry before proceeding.

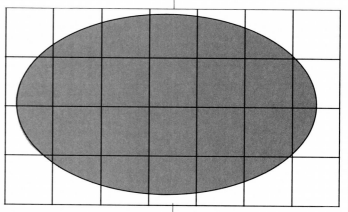

illustration 52 a

1 square = 1 inch

STEP 5

Make a single bow with pale green ribbon around kitty's neck (see page 27). Trim streamer ends in an inverted "V" shape.

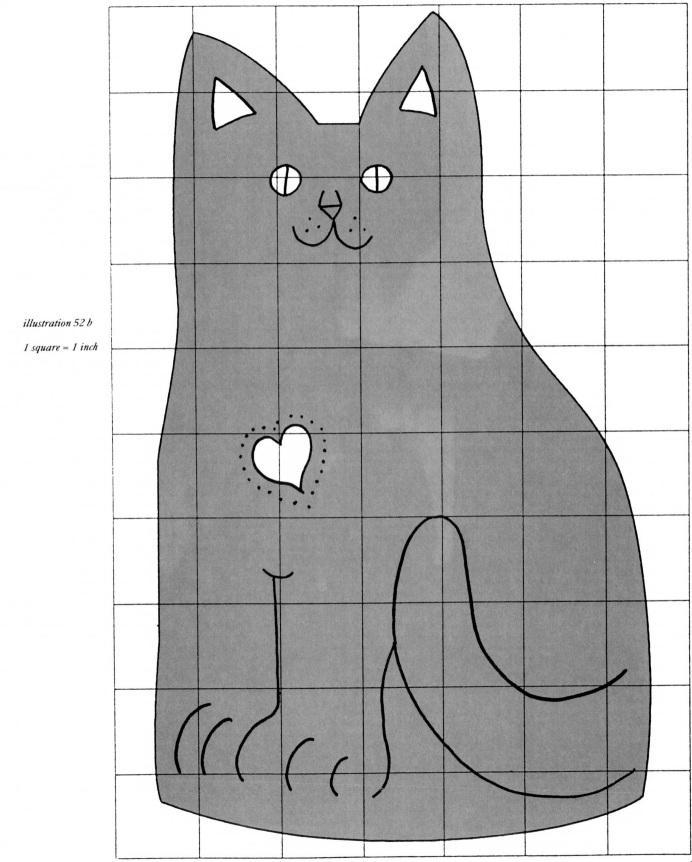

illustration 52 b

1 square = 1 inch

FATHER'S DAY

For all the seasons of life, we keep memories of time spent with Father in a sacred place in our hearts. For teaching us about fishing, for pony rides and for protecting us from harm. For caring, strength, and for working so very hard to give us a beautiful life, we say "Thank You."

Father gives up so much territory to the decorating fashions of the day. Present him with a hand-painted box for his own keepsakes. For a most welcome gift, tuck in a gift certificate (see page 144), perhaps lunch for two.

FATHER'S DAY STATIONERY BOX

MATERIALS:

1 blank canvas stationery box

Sepia, country blue, and metallic gold acrylic paint

Shader brush

Natural sea sponge

Water

Two 3x3-inch tan ultrasuede squares

1 Dresden gold paper lion

Fine-tipped fabric pen

Ruler

Scissors

White craft glue

Glue gun/glue sticks

STEP 1
Open box and paint a wash of metallic gold paint (see page 33) to box sides (the area that resembles pages of a book). Allow paint to dry before proceeding.

STEP 2
Paint all outside surfaces with blue paint. Allow paint to dry before proceeding.

STEP 3
Lightly sponge a pattern of sepia paint on top surface (see page 32). Allow paint to dry before proceeding.

STEP 4
Using ruler and fabric pen, draw a diagonal line, from corner to corner, on each ultrasuede square. Cut on line to create four triangles.

STEP 5
With craft glue, apply triangle pieces to the corners of the top surface.

STEP 6
With hot glue, secure gold lion to the center of the box top.

Designed to be coordinated with Father's stationery box, here is a frame to display the smiles he loves to see.

FATHER'S DAY PHOTO FRAME

MATERIALS:

1 blank canvas folding frame

Sepia, country blue, and metallic gold acrylic paint

Shader brush

Natural sea sponge

1 tan ultrasuede strip cut to fit inside of photo-frame spine

Scissors

White craft glue

STEP 1

Paint photo-frame rectangles with country blue paint. Allow paint to dry before proceeding.

STEP 2

Paint reverse side of folding frame with sepia paint. Using sepia paint, carefully paint around blue-painted areas. Allow paint to dry before proceeding.

STEP 3

Lightly sponge a pattern of gold paint to front and back of frame (see page 32). Allow paint to dry before proceeding. Glue ultrasuede strip to center section between blue photograph holders.

Present Father with a personalized desk clock cleverly covered with marbled paper.

TIME FOR DAD

MATERIALS:

1 unpainted wooden clock with movements

Deep gray, brown, and country blue acrylic paint

Shader brush

1 sheet of blue/brown/cream marbled paper

Tracing paper

Medium-hard pencil

Scissors

Spray adhesive

STEP 1

Remove clock movements and set aside. (Clocks made for crafting usually have pop-out movements.)

STEP 2

Paint top of clock surface and feet with deep gray paint. Paint sides and back with blue paint. Paint edges and base with brown paint. Allow paint to dry.

STEP 3

Make a pattern for clockface by drawing around shape on tracing paper. Cut out pattern.

STEP 4

Place pattern on wrong side of marbled paper. Draw around shape and cut out. Apply spray adhesive to wrong side of paper. Press paper into place. Replace clock movements.

GIFTS FOR THE GARDENER

Roses ramble over the wood fence, and primroses and forget-me-nots nod in the shady spots. Each hour spent in the garden is an hour to remember what life is all about.

This basket for gardening friends to carry seeds for the summers' bloom makes a very personal gift. Paint tool handles with bright colors so they can be spotted easily in the garden.

GARDENER'S BASKET

MATERIALS:

One 12x4x3½-inch natural basket with long handle

⅔ yard of 1-inch-wide burgundy, white and gray tartan French wired ribbon

1 yard of ¼-inch-wide burgundy silk ribbon

2 small painted strawberry clay fruit ornaments

1 each of small painted lemon and pear painted clay fruit ornaments

Glue gun/glue sticks

STEP 1

With hot glue, secure one end of tartan ribbon to inside base of basket handle. Wrap ribbon in a spiral motion around handle. Glue loose ribbon end to inside base of basket handle.

STEP 2

Make a 6-loop bow of tartan ribbon, 8 inches wide overall, with long streamers (see page 27). Trim streamer ends in an inverted "V" shape. Glue bow off-center to basket handle.

STEP 3

Cut silk ribbon into uneven lengths. Tie clay ornaments to ends of ribbon. Glue other end of ribbon to handle under bow.

TOOLS FOR THE GARDENER

MATERIALS:

1 cultivator with wooden handle

1 trowel with wooden handle

1 transplanter with wooden handle

Clear orange, bright red, and spring green acrylic paint

¼ yard of 1-inch-wide blue, white and gray tartan French wired ribbon

½ yard of 1-inch-wide yellow, and white tartan French wired ribbon

Shader brush

Artist's varnish

STEP 1
Paint cultivator handle with orange paint, trowel handle with red paint, and transplanter handle with green paint. Apply two or three even coats. Allow paint to dry.

STEP 2
Seal handles with artist's varnish (see page 31).

STEP 3
Cut yellow and white ribbon in half. Thread one piece of ribbon through each hole in tool handle. Make bows (see page 27).

GARDENER'S APRON

MATERIALS:

1⅔ yards of medium canvas

12 inches of strong woven beige nylon braid

4 self-grip fastening dots

Red and green acrylic paint

Round brush

Liner brush

Red and green iron-on transfer pens

Ruler

Scissors

Pins

Beige thread and needle

Iron

STEP 1
Enlarge patterns, illustrations 54, 55, and 56, to full size (see page 34). Pin patterns to canvas and cut out pieces.

STEP 2
Take 1 semicircle piece and make a ¼-inch double fold along curved edge. Double fold will be to the front of apron. Press well. Machine-stitch all the way around. Set this piece aside.

STEP 3
Fold straight edge of second semicircle down 2 inches and press. Stitch ¼ inch from top edge all the way across. Stitch ½ inch down from first seam all the way across. Stitch 1¼ inches down from second seam all the way across.

STEP 4
Fold under ¼ inch on straight edges of both front pocket pieces and press. If desired, finish raw edges on top with double fold. Stitch folds into place. Position and pin pockets to smaller semicircle, aligning curved edges.

STEP 5
Position semicircle with pockets on larger semicircle, aligning all curves. Sew all pieces together, allowing a generous ¼ inch.

STEP 6
Stitch pocket into place. Continue stitching to top edge of hemmed semicircle to form two pockets. Repeat for second pocket.

STEP 7
Fold apron tie in half lengthwise and press well. Fold all raw edges under ½ inch and press well. Center apron between folds of tie, ½ inch deep. Stitch into place, allowing ½ inch unstitched at each end for finishing.

STEP 8
To finish, stitch apron tie edges closed.

STEP 9
Transfer tulip pattern, illustration 63, page 107, to front of center pocket (see page 34). Paint dotted area with red paint and stem and leaves with green paint. Allow undotted flower area to remain natural canvas. Allow paint to dry completely.

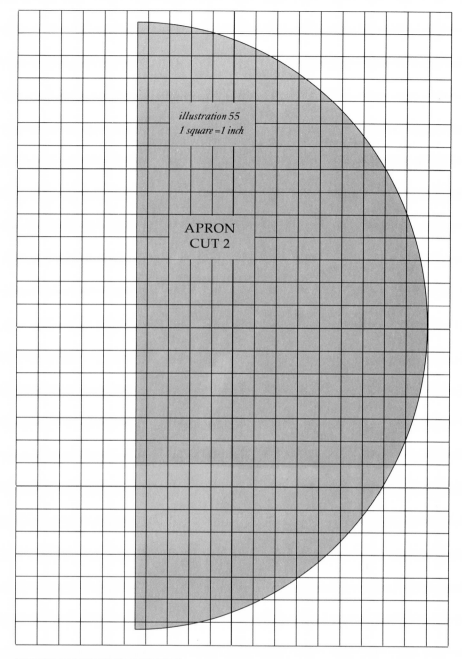

illustration 54
1 square =1 inch

APRON TIE
CUT 1

illustration 55
1 square =1 inch

APRON
CUT 2

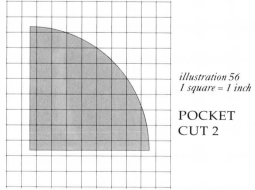

illustration 56
1 square = 1 inch

POCKET
CUT 2

INDEPENDENCE DAY GIFTS

Fireworks, home-cooked treats, and friends all together is reason enough to craft a hostess gift or two. Always enough potato salad and never enough sparklers, but on this early summer's eve, the celebration of liberty and friends fills the heart with gratitude and pride.

What a lovely gift for Dad to place in the tree he planted many years ago! And what a fortunate little bird family to move into a hand-painted log cabin!

LOG CABIN BIRDHOUSE

MATERIALS:

1 log cabin birdhouse

Bright red, barn red, cream, ultramarine blue, and metallic gold acrylic paint

Crackle medium

Shader brush

Round brush

Artist's varnish

STEP 1

With shader brush paint chimney with blue paint and roof with gold paint. Paint cabin logs alternating bright red and cream paint. Paint porch roof and porch with blue paint, base of cabin with red paint, and door frame and porch posts with gold paint. Allow paint to dry before proceeding.

STEP 2

Apply an even coat of crackle medium to all surfaces (see page 33). Allow to set completely.

STEP 3

Paint chimney cream, cabin logs and porch posts with red paint. Paint roof, door frame and cabin base with blue paint. Paint red cabin logs, porch roof and porch with cream paint. As paint dries, cracks will form, exposing base-coat colors. If using outdoors, varnish birdhouse with artist's varnish (see page 31).

Arrange red, white, and blue flowers for the hostess. She will remember your kindness and the occasion all summer long.

FOURTH OF JULY ARRANGEMENT

MATERIALS:

One 8x4x4-inch banded straight-edged twig basket

Round brush

White and blue-gray acrylic paint

One 7x3¹/₂x3-inch block florist's oasis

Large handful green sphagnum moss

1 bunch dried wheat

1 large bunch dried lavender

1 bunch glycerin-preserved baby's breath

10 dried or freeze-dried white rosebuds

5 stems small deep red dried-look silk roses

18 dried bachelor's buttons

Wire cutter

Glue gun/glue sticks

STEP 1

Spray basket with warm water to saturate. Paint twig sections with a wash of white paint (see page 33). Allow paint to dry before proceeding. While basket is drying, trim wheat stems evenly. Trim lavender spikes 2 inches shorter than dried wheat. Trim silk rose wires 4 to 5 inches.

STEP 2

Paint basket bands with blue-gray paint. Allow paint to dry.

STEP 3

With hot glue, secure oasis in basket. Place moss on top of oasis to cover completely.

STEP 4

Insert wheat into center of oasis to form a 5x3-inch rectangle. Encircle wheat with a thick band of lavender spikes. Create a ruff around the lavender with baby's breath. Glue bachelor's buttons and roses among baby's breath, distributing colors evenly.

These trivets are simple to make in red, white and blue. Scent lightly with lemon verbena for freshness. Adapt this project to any season by substituting fabrics and herbs of your choice.

SUMMER HOSTESS TRIVETS

MATERIALS FOR ONE TRIVET:

Two 8-inch squares patriotic print fabric

One 8-inch square of cotton batting

Dried lemon verbena

Fabric marker

Ruler

Coordinating thread and needle

Iron

STEP 1

Position right sides of fabric together, placing batting on top. Stitch 3 sides of the square. Turn right sides out and press.

STEP 2

Sprinkle lemon verbena inside. Fold in edges and slip-stitch closed (see illustration 57). Add lace, rickrack or picot-edged trim as desired.

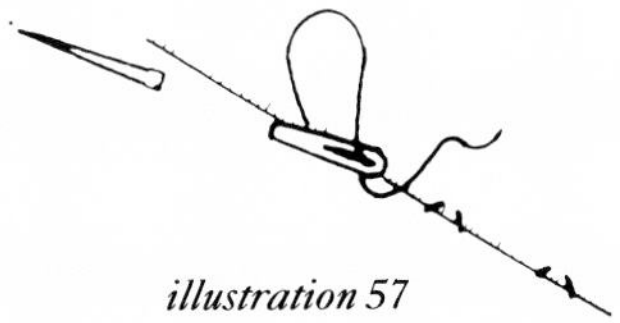

illustration 57

SPECIAL TIP

Make a similar chalkboard by buying a ready-made chalkboard at your craft store. Transfer the apple and leaf patterns provided. Then simply paint designs in coordinating colors.

BACK-TO-SCHOOL GIFTS

September brings drifts of leaves, cinnamon sticks in apple cider and the arrival of the big yellow school bus. It's a time, too, for creativity and crafting. Children will love having an art kit of their very own.

ART BASKET

MATERIALS:

1 wooden bun basket with handle

Medium blue, medium green, light orange, soft red, and cream acrylic paint

Red and green squeeze-bottle fabric paint

Shader brush

1 square red felt

1 square green felt

½ yard of ⅝-inch-wide embroidered ribbon in bright colors

One 8x8-inch square fabric

3 ladybug buttons

Scissors

Pinking or scalloping shears

Glue gun/glue sticks

STEP 1

Paint handle top and basket ends (inside and out) with cream paint. Paint handle sides with alternating colors of paint. Paint top rim of basket with green paint. Paint slats alternating colors of paint. Allow paint to dry.

STEP 2

Transfer apple pattern, illustration 58, 4 times to red felt (see page 34). Using scissors, cut out apple shapes. Transfer leaf pattern, illustration 59, 4 times to green felt (see page 34). With shears, cut out leaves. Glue two apples and leaves to each side of basket. Dot red and green fabric paint on apples and leaves to decorate. Glue ladybugs to leaves.

STEP 3

If desired, trim edges of fabric square with pinking or scalloping shears. Place fabric square in basket to line.

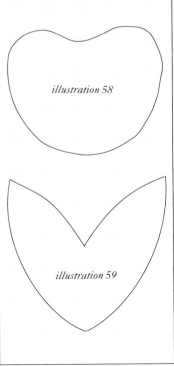

illustration 58

illustration 59

ART AND CRAFT APRON

MATERIALS:

¾ yard of natural canvas

¼ yard of heavy muslin

3½ yards of double-fold bias tape

¼ yard of ⅝-inch-wide embroidered ribbon

1 square red felt

1 square green felt

3 ladybug buttons

2 self-grip fastening tape dots

Pins

Coordinating thread and needle

Scissors

Pinking or scalloping shears

Glue gun/glue sticks

STEP 1
Enlarge patterns, illustrations 60, 61, 62, and to full size (see page 34). Pin to canvas and cut out 1 body pattern and 2 of each pocket pattern.

STEP 2
Beginning at one underarm and ending at the other, fold bias tape over edge of canvas around lower section of apron body. Topstitch bias tape to canvas. Trim tape. Repeat with straight-edged neckline and trim tape.

STEP 3
To form apron ties and neck loop, stitch approximately 18 inches of tape closed. Do not cut tape.

STEP 4
Place bottom of apron underarm into tape fold. Continue to stitch tape over armhole. When top edge of armhole is reached, stitch approximately 18 inches of tape closed to form neck loop. Do not cut tape.

STEP 5
Place top of remaining armhole into tape fold. Continue to stitch tape down over other armhole. When bottom of armhole is reached continue stitching approximately 18 inches of tape closed to form second tie and trim.

STEP 6
With wrong sides of canvas together, pin like-sized pocket pieces together. Edge-finish all sides of pocket by turning ¼ inch outside and stitching along raw edges. Turn right side out, turning under raw edges. Press.

STEP 7
Pin pockets to apron and stitch into place (see photograph, page 104), allowing ¼-inch seam.

STEP 8
Transfer apple pattern, illustration 58, 2 times to red felt (see page 34). With scissors, cut out apple shapes. Transfer leaf pattern, illustration 59, 4 times to green felt. With shears, cut out leaves. Glue leaves to apples. Glue ladybug buttons to leaves. Attach apples to apron pockets using fastening dots.

STEP 9
Cut two 3-inch pieces of embroidered ribbon. Stitch loops of ribbon to large apron pocket to hold scissors and paintbrush.

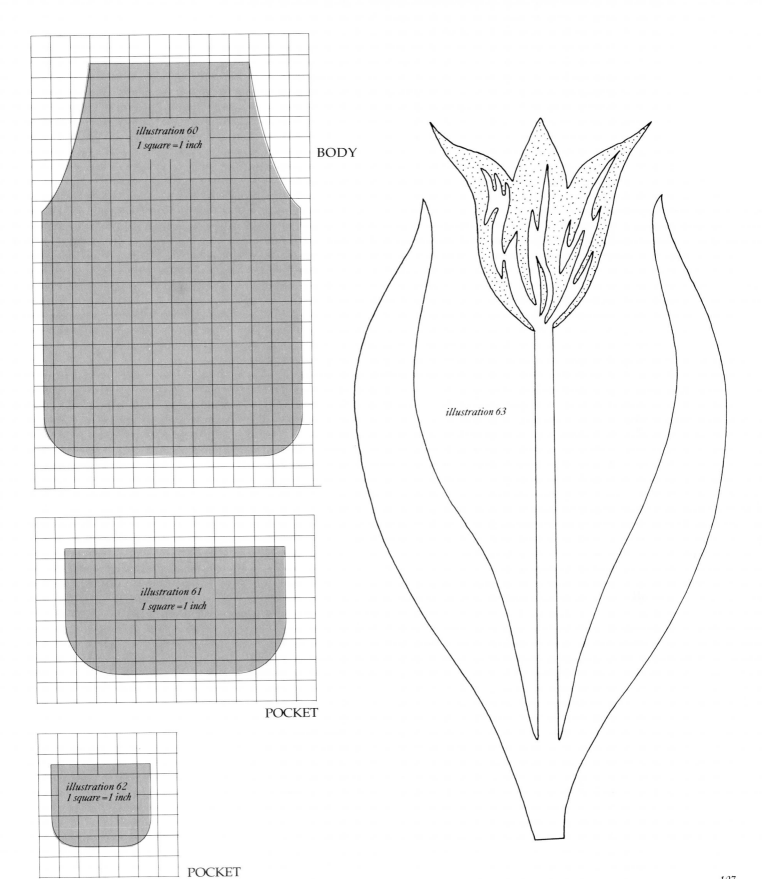

illustration 60
1 square = 1 inch

BODY

illustration 61
1 square = 1 inch

POCKET

illustration 62
1 square = 1 inch

POCKET

illustration 63

AUTUMN FRIENDSHIP GIFTS

Summer has passed and it is time for tea and stories with a dear friend. In all our lives, only a handful of people truly know us, and there are never enough times together to express our gratitude.

ROSE TOPIARY

MATERIALS:

One 4-inch-diameter embossed clay cachepot

Metallic pale gold and blue-gray acrylic paint

Round brush

One 3½-inch-diameter plastic foam ball

3 ounces scarlet rosebuds

Three 6-inch small twigs

Plastic foam cut to fit cachepot

Green sphagnum moss

Glue gun/glue sticks

STEP 1

Lightly wash a small amount of blue-gray paint over clay cachepot (see page 33). Allow paint to dry. Follow with gold metallic paint to highlight cachepot. Allow paint to dry.

STEP 2

With glue, secure plastic foam shape in cachepot. Cover foam completely with moss. Secure moss in place with glue. Set aside.

STEP 3

Hold twigs together and push into foam ball, securing with glue. Holding twigs in hand, glue rosebuds, tightly spaced, to foam ball.

STEP 4

Insert twigs into plastic foam base, pressing firmly.

Oh, to be miniature for just a short time and linger beneath a tree of roses on a mossy knoll! Someone dear will treasure your thoughtfulness. Topiaries can be scented by dabbing damask rose oil onto moss.

Potpourri displayed in bowls exposes only one layer of scent to the air, but fixed to a wreath, all petals and leaves perfume the air. To freshen the scent, simply add a little essential oil to the back of the wreath.

WREATH OF POTPOURRI

MATERIALS:

One 6½-inch round twig wreath

5 cups potpourri

1½ yards of ¼-inch-wide navy silk ribbon

Glue gun/glue sticks

STEP 1

Working in small sections, cover front and sides of wreath with hot glue. Pat on potpourri to cover.

STEP 2

To make hanger, cut a 3-inch piece of ribbon. With hot glue, attach ribbon ends to back of wreath.

STEP 3

Make an 8-loop bow with double streamers (see page 27). Glue bow to upper left section of wreath.

In just a few moments, this exquisite decorated gift tin is ready to be filled with sweetly-scented blossoms.

RIBBONS OF FRANCE

MATERIALS:

One 6½x2½-inch round tin, without lid

1 yard of 4½-inch-wide iridescent violet pleated French wired ribbon

2 yards of 1½-inch-wide antique white with stripes and gold-edged French wired ribbon

4 to 6 cups potpourri

Glue gun/glue sticks

STEP 1

Encircle tin with pleated ribbon, allowing ½ inch extra on bottom for flare. Cut to size. Secure to tin sides with glue (2 inches remain over top of tin to ruffle).

STEP 2

Tie a chain of single knots in antique white knotted ribbon (see page 27). Glue ribbon chain into place around center of pleated ribbon (not center of tin).

STEP 3

With fingers, gently smooth along ribbon wires to create ruffled edges. Fill tin with potpourri.

AUTUMN WREATH PILLOW

MATERIALS:

One 12x12-inch square natural canvas

One 12x12-inch square small autumnal print fabric

Gold, sepia, deep red, plum, rust, forest green, hunter green, Christmas green acrylic paint

1¼ yards of ¼-inch-wide coordinated piping (optional)

Cotton batting or pillow form

Round brush

Liner brush

Gold and green iron-on transfer pens

STEP 1

Transfer wreath pattern, illustration 64, to fabric (see page 34).

STEP 2

Reserve green paints for leaves and stems. Paint flowers and berries with remaining colors, using pleasing combinations. Use round brush for large areas, and liner brush for small berries and outlines. Allow paint to dry before proceeding.

STEP 3

With right sides of canvas and print fabric together, pin piping (if used) between the layers of fabric so rounded edge of piping is toward inside of pillow.

STEP 4

At ends of piping, fold neatly so that ends emerge just outside fabric squares, no more than 1 inch. Machine-stitch around pillow edges with machine foot against edge of piping. Leave 4 to 5 inches open for turning and stuffing. If using pillow form, leave one side completely open.

STEP 5

Turn right sides out and press. Stuff with batting or pillow form. Tuck piping into place and slip-stitch closed (see illustration 65).

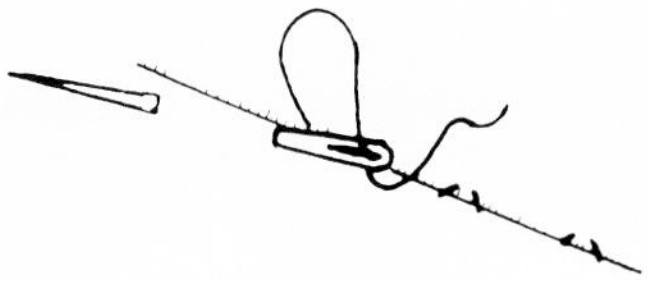

illustration 65

illustration 64

*The look
of needlepoint
need not take
hours to create.
Paint a scrap of
canvas or cotton
and sign your
original!*

FRAMED AUTUMN NOSEGAY

MATERIALS:

One 10x10-inch square natural canvas

Plum, grape, deep red, gold, sepia, rust, forest green, hunter green, and Christmas green acrylic paint

Round brush

Purchased frame with cardboard insert

Glue gun/glue sticks

STEP 1
Transfer pattern, illustration 66, to canvas square (see page 34).

STEP 2
Paint bouquet, reserving green paints for leaves and stems. Paint flowers and berries with remaining colors of paint in pleasing combinations. Use round brush for large areas and liner brush for berries and outlines. Allow paint to dry before proceeding.

STEP 3
Center painting on cardboard frame insert. Fold edges around cardboard and secure with hot glue. Place canvas in frame.

illustration 66

HALLOWEEN ARRANGEMENT

Paint a wash of gold paint on artificial pumpkins and real garlic (see page 33) and arrange a basket of petals and moss for a beautiful Halloween arrangement.

HALLOWEEN HARVEST GIFTS

During autumn days the heart opens in extraordinary ways. As we craft, the leaves fall and the seasons change once again. On a special fall evening, warm fires welcome ghosts and fairies quoting poetry for sweet rewards.

Why leave all the leaf painting to elves? Join in and make your mark on the colors of fall. Children will enjoy collecting and painting leaves for a wreath gift.

HALLOWEEN WREATH

MATERIALS:

One 11-inch cinnamon-scented twig heart wreath

18 small to medium gold and red glycerin-preserved oak leaves

7 to 8 collected dried leaves

Metallic light gold, metallic copper, metallic dark gold, teal, moss green, pale orange and gold acrylic paint

Crackle medium

Round brush

Mixing plate and water

30 autumn acorns and berries

1 medium jack-o'-lantern bell

1½ yards of 1½-inch-wide rust organdy ribbon

6 inches rust yarn

Glue gun/glue sticks

STEP 1

Apply a coat of crackle medium to bell. Allow to dry before proceeding. Paint bell with gold paint. Allow to dry before proceeding. Apply a second coat of crackle medium to bell. Allow crackle to dry before proceeding. Paint orange paint over gold (see page 33). Set aside to dry.

STEP 2

Using varying mixes of metallic, teal and green paints, paint leaf surfaces, adding details to edges and natural leaf lines. Set aside to dry.

STEP 3

Glue groups of glycerin-preserved oak leaves to wreath, spacing evenly. Distribute and glue acorns and berries among leaves. Glue painted leaves to oak leaves distributing evenly.

STEP 4

Make a 6-loop bow, 6 inches wide overall (see page 27). Trim streamer ends to an inverted "V" shape. Glue bow to heart center. Using rust yarn, hang bell beneath bow. To make a wreath hanger, see tip on page 60.

GIFTS FOR THE COOK

Take a moment to remember the warm apple pie, served with a beaming smile by Grandmother, and those little pie dough scraps, baked with butter and cinnamon—food for the soul. Those who brightened our lives with delicious treats surely need a heartfelt gift of gratitude.

HERB AND SPICE LABELS

Show appreciation for the cook with a contribution of herbs and spices, custom-blended and labeled. Photocopy this label page, hand-color borders, and affix to bottles with white craft glue.

Permission granted to photocopy this page for personal use only.

HERBS AND SPICES RECIPES

All recipes call for dried herbs and spices.

HERBES DE PROVENCE

Equal proportions of:

🌿 *Basil*

🌿 *Fennel*

🌿 *French thyme*

🌿 *Lavender*

🌿 *Marjoram*

🌿 *Rosemary*

Tie above ingredients in cheesecloth or muslin bag, or throw a pinch into soups, casseroles, vegetarian dishes such as ratatouille as well as into soft cheeses for a different taste.

BOUQUET GARNI

🌿 *2 sprigs parsley*

🌿 *2 sprigs thyme*

🌿 *1 bay leaf*

Tie above ingredients in cheesecloth or muslin bag. Add to casseroles, stews, sauces, and soups.

APPLE PIE SPICES

Equal proportions of:

🌿 *Cloves*

🌿 *Cinnamon*

🌿 *Allspice*

🌿 *Dried, grated orange peel*

Mix together above ingredients. Sprinkle a small amount over apples just before baking pie.

HERBS FOR CHEESES

Equal proportions of:

🌿 *Dried parsley*

🌿 *Thyme*

🌿 *Basil*

🌿 *Caraway*

2 pinches of:

🌿 *Fennel*

🌿 *Lemon pepper*

Mix together above ingredients. Add a small amount to soft cheeses for a delicious snack.

MULLED CIDER SPICES

Equal proportions of:

🌿 *Cloves*

🌿 *Cinnamon*

🌿 *Allspice*

🌿 *Mace*

Mix together above ingredients. Add a small amount to apple juice or cider before warming.

MINT TEA

Equal proportions of:

🌿 *Dried peppermint leaves*

🌿 *Dried spearmint leaves*

🌿 *Dried lemon balm*

Mix together above ingredients. Store in a tea tin. Add a small amount to a cup of boiling water for mint tea.

ACORN KITCHEN BASKET

MATERIALS:

One 9x6x1⅔-inch oval wooden basket with handle

Teal, barn red, hunter green, moss green, rust, burnt sienna, dusty rose, and cream acrylic paint

Shader brush

Liner brush

Masking tape

Ruler

STEP 1

With shader brush, paint underside of handle and basket interior with teal paint. Allow paint to dry before proceeding.

STEP 2

Paint top of basket handle with barn red paint. Paint remaining basket surfaces with cream paint. Allow paint to dry before proceeding.

STEP 3

Measure ½ inch from top and bottom edges of basket. Place masking tape over center section, exposing the ½-inch band at top and bottom. Do not press tape down firmly. Paint borders with hunter green paint. Allow paint to dry. Gently remove tape. Touch up edges with cream paint, if necessary. Allow paint to dry before proceeding.

STEP 4

Transfer acorn motif, illustration 67, to basket around cream section (see page 34). Trace pattern several times to keep lines clean and sharp.

STEP 5

Reserve green paints for leaves and stems. Paint acorns and heart motif with rust, burnt sienna, and dusty rose paint. Use shader brush for large areas, and liner brush for outlines and details.

illustration 67

WREATH OF BAY

MATERIALS:

One 9-inch round straw wreath

8 ounces dried whole bay leaves

12 slices dried oranges

7 to 8 slices dried apple

Nine 2-inch pieces cinnamon sticks

5 to 6 whole star anise

Small bunch pepperberries

Glue gun/glue sticks

STEP 1

Begin wreath by gluing bay leaves to front in a single-layer fan shape (see illustration 68). Continue fan shaped-layers on top of first layer until wreath is covered, overlapping slightly (see illustration 69).

illustration 68

STEP 2

Glue 4 groupings of apples, oranges, and cinnamon sticks to bay wreath, spacing evenly. Add berries and star anise to upper left grouping. To make a wreath hanger, see tip on page 60.

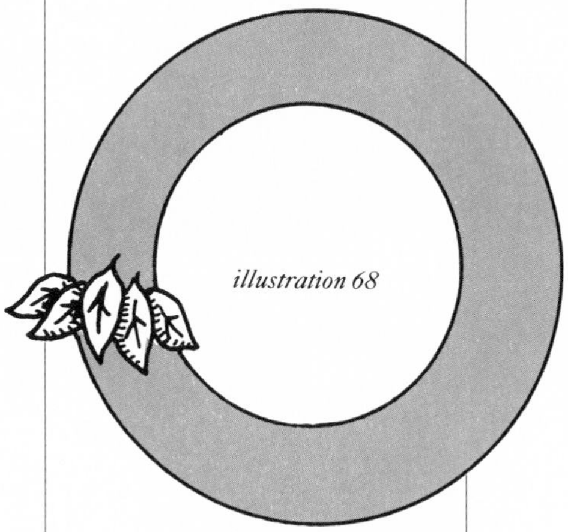

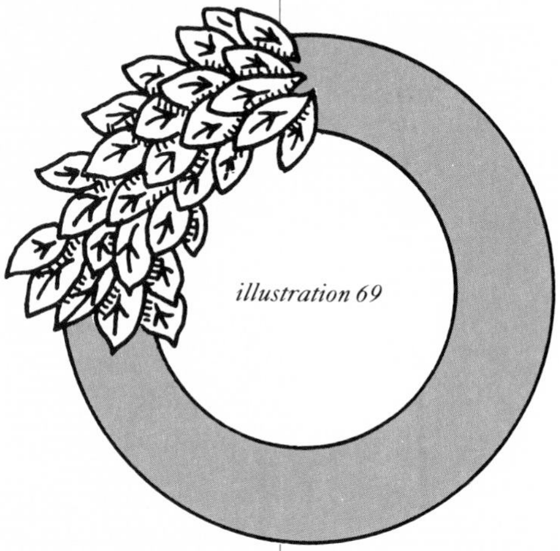

illustration 69

THANKSGIVING GIFTS

Puffs of white rise from chimney tops as Thanksgiving scents and the sound of familiar voices fill the air. This holiday of sharing and gratitude is a perfect occasion to create crafted gifts of rich texture and autumn colors.

This project can be adapted for use as Christmas ornaments by substituting small artificial apples and cinnamon mixed with spices. Tie apples to the tree with green wired bows.

POTPOURRI NESTED FRUITS

MATERIALS:

A selection of large, richly-colored artificial fruit

3 cups potpourri

Small bowl

Glue gun/glue sticks

Place potpourri in bowl. Apply glue to bottom half of fruit. Press and roll glued section in potpourri.

HARVEST TOPIARY

MATERIALS:

One 7x5-inch embossed terra-cotta pot

Plastic foam cut to fit pot securely, round top of foam to rise 2 inches above rim of pot at center

Green sphagnum moss

One 8-inch-diameter plastic foam ball

5 cups Autumn Harvest Potpourri (see recipe, page 23)

60 acorns

60 variegated, peach like berries

30 small artificial plums

30 small artificial fruits

24 green and plum velveteen oak leaves

40 small glycerin-preserved oak leaves

3 yards of ¾-inch-wide copper curly paper ribbon

Three 12-inch sturdy, straight twigs

20 spikes dried lavender

Large mixing bowl

Glue gun/glue sticks

STEP 1
With glue, secure plastic foam shape in pot. Hold twigs together and push 4 inches into foam ball, securing with glue.

STEP 2
Cover foam completely with moss. With glue, secure moss in place. Glue two preserved oak leaves to moss. Trim lavender spikes to 3 inches and glue in moss, forming a small wild lavender garden.

STEP 3
Place potpourri in large mixing bowl. Apply hot glue to a small section of plastic foam ball. Roll and press foam ball into potpourri. Continue adding glue and potpourri until foam ball is covered.

STEP 4
Press potpourri ball firmly onto twigs, securing with glue.

STEP 5
With hot glue, attach individual fruits, berries, acorns and leaves to topiary.

STEP 6
Unroll paper ribbon and drape around tree, allowing loops to form naturally. Secure ribbon to tree with dots of glue.

Set the table with lights, a flame burning for each guest. They will have a holiday memento to take home that will glow throughout the winter months.

THANKSGIVING FAVORS

MATERIALS:

1 square gold felt

½ of 2½-inch-diameter plastic foam ball

1 small wooden candle holder

Metallic copper and metallic gold acrylic paint

Round brush

2 small cinnamon sticks

2 eucalyptus pods

5 small pinecones

Green sphagnum moss

Small amount oakmoss

Natural sea sponge

⅓ yard of ⅝-inch-wide iridescent yellow with pink edge French wired ribbon

Small beeswax candles

Felt pen

Glue gun/glue sticks

STEP 1

With round brush, paint candle holder with metallic copper paint. Allow paint to dry. Sponge on gold paint to create pattern (see page 32). Allow paint to dry.

STEP 2

Place foam ball, flat side down, on felt. Draw around shape. Cut out and glue into place on flat side of foam ball. Press candle holder onto rounded side of ball, creating a flattened surface. Glue candle holder into place.

STEP 3

Glue sphagnum moss to exposed sides of plastic foam ball. Glue oakmoss to front of foam ball. Add cones, pods, and cinnamon sticks to decorate.

STEP 4

Make a single bow of French wired ribbon (see page 27). Trim streamer ends to an inverted "V" shape. Glue bow to front of arrangement. Add a beeswax candle to each candle holder.

GIFTS FOR CHRISTMAS

As the days grow shorter and snow blankets the garden, thoughts turn to home and holidays with those we love. This season, create time away from shopping schedules to craft gifts. There is an extraordinary feeling of peace on earth as we return to working with our hands.

STRAWBERRY ORNAMENTS

MATERIALS:

½ yard scarlet moiré

Cotton batting

Scarlet thread and needle

2 yards of ½-inch-wide forest green with gold edge French wired ribbon

Twelve 1½-inch square brass-filigree jewelry findings

Thin brass craft wire

Scissors

Wire cutter

Glue gun/glue sticks

STEP 1
Transfer pattern, illustration 70, to fabric 12 times (see page 34). Cut out.

STEP 2
Sew a running stitch along edges of oval (see illustration 71). Gather oval partway. Place a dot of hot glue at center of bottom and pinch fabric together to form a point. Pull thread to close pouch slightly. Fill each strawberry with batting. Pull thread to gather completely. Stitch over closure to reinforce.

illustration 71

STEP 3
Bend each filigree square loosely in half to form a pointed cap. Glue a filigree square to top of each strawberry. Cut forest green ribbon into 6-inch pieces.

Make a small single bow with each piece of ribbon, securing center with a twist of wire (see page 27). Trim streamer ends. Glue a bow to top of each filigree cap.

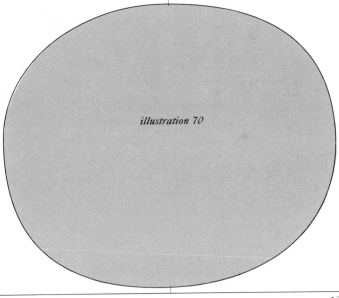

illustration 70

LARGE STRAWBERRY

Craft larger moiré strawberries for trees and wreaths with same materials as small strawberries, noting these changes:

2 brass-filigree jewelry findings for each large strawberry

1 yard of ½-inch-wide forest green with gold edge French wired ribbon for each large strawberry

STEP 1
Enlarge pattern, illustration 72, to full size (see page 34). Transfer pattern to fabric. Cut out.

STEP 2
Follow Step 2 for small Strawberry Ornaments (see page 129).

STEP 3
Bend filigree pieces to curve slightly and glue one to top of each strawberry at center.

STEP 4
Cut a 4-inch piece of ribbon. Twist several times to form a rolled, thin ribbon strand. To form hanger, glue ribbon ends to top of strawberry.

STEP 5
Use remaining ribbon to make a 6-loop bow, 3 inches wide overall, with two streamers (see page 27). Trim streamer ends in an inverted "V" shape. Glue bow to top of strawberry or where filigree pieces meet.

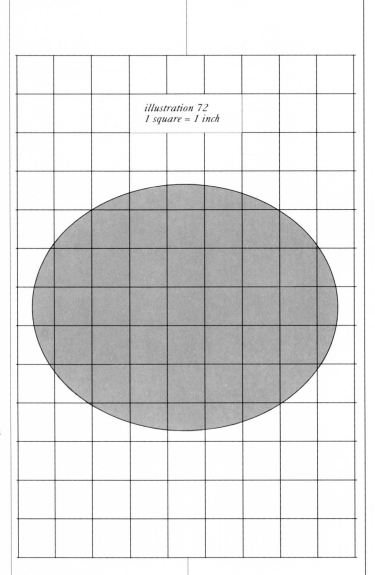

illustration 72
1 square = 1 inch

STRAWBERRIES OF WINTER TOPIARY

MATERIALS:

One 13-inch plastic-foam cone-shaped topiary tree form

1 bag bright green Spanish moss

One 6-inch clay bulb pot

2 handfuls green sphagnum moss

Metallic pale gold acrylic paint

Shader brush

1½ yards of 1-inch-wide deep red, gold-edged, gold-embossed fleur-de-lis pattern French wired ribbon

4 yards of ⅜-inch-wide deep red French wired ribbon

¾ yard of ⅝-inch-wide burgundy Christmas floral pattern French wired ribbon

Strawberry Ornaments (see project, page 129)

Glue gun/glue sticks

STEP 1
Paint a wash of pale gold paint on pot (see page 33). Allow paint to dry before proceeding.

STEP 2
With hot glue, secure tree base in pot. Glue on sphagnum moss to cover base. Encircle top rim of pot with fleur-de-lis ribbon. Cut to size. Glue into place. Use remaining ribbon to make a double bow, 4 inches wide overall, with two streamers (see page 27). Trim streamer ends in an inverted "V" shape. Glue bow to center of ribbon band.

STEP 3
Working in small sections, glue Spanish moss to tree form to cover completely.

STEP 4
Cut ⅜-inch-wide red ribbon into 10-inch sections. Make pretty single bows with each ribbon and set aside. Using ⅝-inch-wide burgundy Christmas print ribbon, make an 8-loop bow, 3½ inches wide overall, with four streamers (see page 27). Trim streamer ends in an inverted "V" shape. Glue printed ribbon bow to top of tree (see page 27).

STEP 5
With hot glue, secure deep red ribbon bows and Strawberry Ornaments to tree, evenly distributing.

Brass charms, easily painted, adorn a heart of pine for a very special gift. This wreath ships easily and will be treasured for many years.

CHRISTMAS CHARM WREATH

MATERIALS:

One 9-inch pine heart wreath

Brass charms:

  2 large bird-shaped

  2 patterned bow-shaped

  1 French horn-shaped

  1 heart-shaped

  1 heart-shaped locket

  1 filigree heart-shaped locket

  1 cherub-shaped

  1 angel-shaped with flowers

  1 crescent moon-shaped

Metallic blue, red and gold acrylic paint

Acrylic glaze crystal, with sparkles

Round brush

1¼ yards of 1-inch-wide deep red with gold edging and dots French wired ribbon

Small bunch preserved miniature baby's breath

Glue suitable for metal

Glue gun/glue sticks

STEP 1
Prepare charms
(see page 34).

STEP 2
Paint charms with mixes of paint colors. Allow paint to dry and seal with acrylic glaze crystal (see page 34). Allow glaze to dry completely.

STEP 3
With glue for metal, attach charms to wreath, reserving filigree heart-shaped charm and cherub-shaped charm for center of bow. With hot glue, attach small sprigs of baby's breath throughout wreath.

STEP 4
Make a 4-loop bow, 4 inches wide overall, with streamers (see page 27). Trim streamer ends in an inverted "V" shape. With hot glue, attach bow to center of wreath. With glue for metal, attach filigree heart-shaped charm and cherub-shaped charm to center of bow. To make a wreath hanger, see tip on page 60.

OLD WORLD CHRISTMAS WREATH

MATERIALS:

One 12-inch-diameter straw wreath

12 to 15 European cotton wadding fruit ornaments

12 large natural or artificial walnuts

1 package German hoarfrost (antique silica flakes)

1 large bunch preserved dried maidenhair fern

1 large bunch pale green glycerin-preserved peppergrass

1 large bunch natural preserved miniature baby's breath

Metallic dark gold acrylic paint

Round brush

1½ yards of 1½-inch-wide watermelon red organdy ribbon

Glue gun/glue sticks

STEP 1
Paint walnuts with gold paint. While paint is wet, sprinkle hoarfrost on walnuts. Allow paint to dry completely.

STEP 2
Working in small sections, glue fern and peppergrass thickly to front and sides of wreath until straw wreath has been completely covered. Glue fruit ornaments, walnuts and baby's breath to wreath, distributing evenly.

STEP 3
Make a 6-loop bow of organdy ribbon, 6 inches wide overall, with long streamers (see page 27). With hot glue, attach bow to wreath. To make a wreath hanger, see tip on page 60.

illustration 73

SWEET CHRISTMAS BIRD

MATERIALS:

Two 4x4-inch squares wine moiré

Cotton batting

Wine thread and needle

½ yard of ¼-inch-wide gold cord

Gold and variegated metallic rayon or silk thread

¼ yard elasticized gold cord

One 4-inch spun-glass bird tail

Scissors

Glue gun/glue sticks

STEP 1
Transfer pattern, illustration 73, to fabric 2 times (see page 34). Adding ½ inch seam allowance, cut out bird shapes. With right sides together sew fabric, leaving tail section open. Turn inside out and stuff with batting.

STEP 2
Use satin stitch (see illustration 74) and gold thread to create a beak. Add 2 double French knots for eyes (see illustration 75).

STEP 3
Using satin stitch (see illustration 74) with variegated metallic thread, fill in outline of wings (if edges are uneven, cord will cover). Glue cord into place around wing shapes.

STEP 4
Insert bird tail 1 inch into bird body. Secure with hot glue. Finish tail by winding elasticized cord and thread around it several times. Secure cord and thread with hot glue.

STEP 5
To form hanger, with hot glue, secure the ends of elasticized gold cord to the center of bird's back.

illustration 74

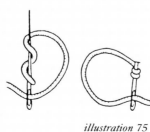

illustration 75

RED VELVET CHRISTMAS SACHET

MATERIALS:

One 7½x7-inch piece red velvet

½ yard of ⅝-inch-wide hunter green with gold bees and gold edging French wired ribbon

¼ yard gold elastic cord

Red thread and needle

STEP 1

Fold fabric with wrong side out. Stitch side and bottom hems to form a bag. Turn top edge down ½ inch and stitch into place. Turn bag right side out.

STEP 2

Fill with Christmas potpourri.

STEP 3

Tie gold elastic cord around bottom of sachet 1 inch above bottom seam. Finish cord by tying a single bow on back (see page 27). Using French wired ribbon make a single bow to close sachet (see page 27).

GREEN VELVET CHRISTMAS SACHET

MATERIALS:

1 piece 8½x15-inch green velvet

1¼ yards of 1-inch-wide deep red, gold-edged and gold-embossed fleur de lis pattern French wired ribbon

Pins

Green thread and needle

Glue gun/glue sticks

STEP 1

Turn under ½ inch fabric on all sides and finish raw edge. Turn up 4½ inches of fabric from bottom edge. Stitch into place. Fold down top flap, allowing ¾ inch of pouch to show.

STEP 2

Cut an 8½-inch piece of ribbon. Allowing ¼ inch of ribbon to turn under, attach to front flap of sachet on diagonal, beginning at lower left (see illustration 76). Glue ribbon ends into place.

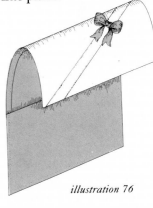

illustration 76

STEP 3

Use remaining ribbon to make a small double loop bow with streamers (see page 27). Trim streamer ends in an inverted "V" shape. Glue bow to diagonal ribbon in top right corner.

LITTLE CHRISTMAS ANGEL

MATERIALS:

Two 6x6-inch squares bridal white or cream soft, fine-textured fabric

White or cream thread and needle

Cotton batting

One 8x3-inch piece antique ecru lace

¼ yard of ½-inch-wide cream lace edging

Scrap of pretty lace trim for collar

Platinum doll hair

11 medium pearls

11 gold glass beads

1 miniature cream open silk rose

1 cranberry triple silk rosette with beads

Black and light pink acrylic paint

Liner brush

One 4-inch round ecru cotton lace doily

¼ yard metallic gold elasticized cord

Fabric marker in light color

Scissors

Glue gun/glue sticks

STEP 1

Transfer angel pattern, illustration 77, to fine fabric (see page 34). Cut out two.

STEP 2

With right sides together, stitch around angel's body, leaving 2 inches open at bottom. Stuff body with batting to desired firmness. Close opening with slip stitch (see illustration 78). Sew a running stitch at neckline (see illustration 79). Gather to form head.

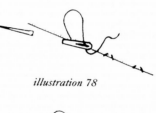

illustration 78

illustration 79

STEP 3

Wrap and smooth largest piece of antique ecru lace around angel, beginning and ending at center back. Glue lace into place. Trim excess. Glue scrap of lace trim into place at neckline. Secure one end of lace edging to shoulder. Bring lace edging down diagonally to center of body. Fold edging to form a "V" shape. Secure with glue. Glue remaining end of edging to shoulder.

STEP 4

Glue cream silk rose at center of collar. Glue triple silk rosette to lace "V" shape to form angel's bouquet. Alternating pearls and glass beads, stitch to lace hemline.

STEP 5

Glue on angel's hair, arranging curls to cover shoulders.

STEP 6

To form wings, tie doily at center with gold cord. Trim excess cord and glue to angel's back. To form hanger, glue a loop of gold cord to angel's back.

STEP 7

Paint eyes with dots of black paint and cheeks with pink paint.

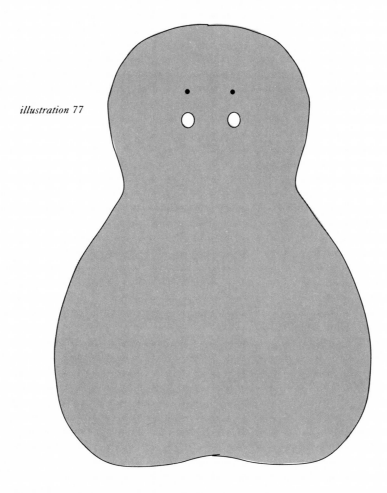

illustration 77

GIFTS FOR PETS

Silver branches dotted with scarlet cardinals and fat little sparrows...
our dear cat sleeps on the chair... the ever-faithful friend naps while we catch up
on letters and cards. We must not forget a gift for that faithful friend.
This project was quite difficult to complete, as our dog Rosie
kept begging for biscuits.

Decorate a wreath with treats for pup using twists of wire—someone will be very pleased!

BISCUITS-FOR-A-FRIEND WREATH

MATERIALS:

One 10-inch diameter willow wreath

Hunter green acrylic paint

Round brush

10 to 12 dog biscuits

Green florist's wire

3 yards of ¼-inch-wide Christmas red paper ribbon

1 yard of 1½-inch-wide Christmas print paper ribbon

Wire cutter

Glue gun/glue sticks

STEP 1

Spray wreath with warm water until saturated. Apply acrylic paint to all surfaces. Allow paint to dry completely.

STEP 2

With florist's wire attach biscuits to wreath. Tie 8-inch pieces of red ribbon around biscuits to conceal wire. Tie ribbon into bows.

STEP 3

Using print ribbon, make a double-loop bow, 5 inches wide overall with streamers (see page 27). Finish streamer ends in an inverted "V" shape. Glue bow to top of wreath. To make a wreath hanger, see tip on page 60.

*Continue
nature's cycle
with treats for
visiting forest friends.
Wire wreaths to trees
and fence posts
for winter months;
perhaps a few
photo opportunities
will result!*

KITTY'S CHRISTMAS COLLAR

MATERIALS:

1 nylon cat collar with thread-through buckle

⅔ yard of ⅝-inch-wide burgundy Christmas floral pattern French wired ribbon

¼ yard of 1½-inch-wide hunter green organdy ribbon

Green thread and needle

2 mouse buttons

2 self-grip fastening tape dots

Glue gun/glue sticks

illustration 80

STEP 1
Place collar on flat surface, right side up. Place wired ribbon, right side up, on top of collar, allowing 1 inch extra at thread-through end. Working in sections, glue ribbon to collar. Thread ribbon through center section of buckle. Turn collar over.

STEP 2
Working in sections, glue ribbon to underside of collar. Trim excess. To finish, fold over 1-inch allowance from top of collar and glue into place on underside.

STEP 3
Create a ruffled pouf of green organdy ribbon by sewing a running stitch along one edge of ribbon and drawing thread to gather ribbon (see illustration 80). Double knot thread. Glue pouf to center of collar.

STEP 4
Using French wired ribbon, make a small single bow with no streamers (see page 27). Glue bow to center of pouf. Glue mouse buttons to bow.

SUNFLOWER WREATH

MATERIALS:

1 sunflower seed head, dried flat, center cut away

9 small whole bay leaves

12 sprigs sweet Annie

9 small pinecones

1 bunch small rose hips

1 yard of ⅜-inch-wide moss green hand-painted rayon taffeta ribbon

Glue gun/glue sticks

STEP 1
Using bay leaves, Sweet Annie, pinecones, and rose hips, glue materials in a pleasing combination to top rim of sunflower head (be sure glue does not come in contact with seed area as it could be harmful if ingested).

STEP 2
Make a small 8-loop bow with streamers (see page 27). Trim streamer ends in an inverted "V" shape. Glue into place on top rim of wreath. To make a wreath hanger, see tip on page 60.

BIRD FEEDER

MATERIALS:

1 wooden high-rise birdhouse

Forest green, evergreen, brown, barn red, cream acrylic paint

Shader brush

Liner brush

Matte finish acrylic or artist's varnish

STEP 1

With shader brush paint roof with forest green paint, house with cream paint, house platform with evergreen paint, post with brown paint and base with barn red paint. Each section will require 2 or 3 coats of paint for outdoor use. Allow paint to dry between coats and before proceeding.

STEP 2

Transfer holly pattern, illustration 81, to house front (see page 141). With liner brush, paint holly leaves with forest green paint and berries with barn red paint.

STEP 3

Seal house well with varnish for outdoor use (see page 31).

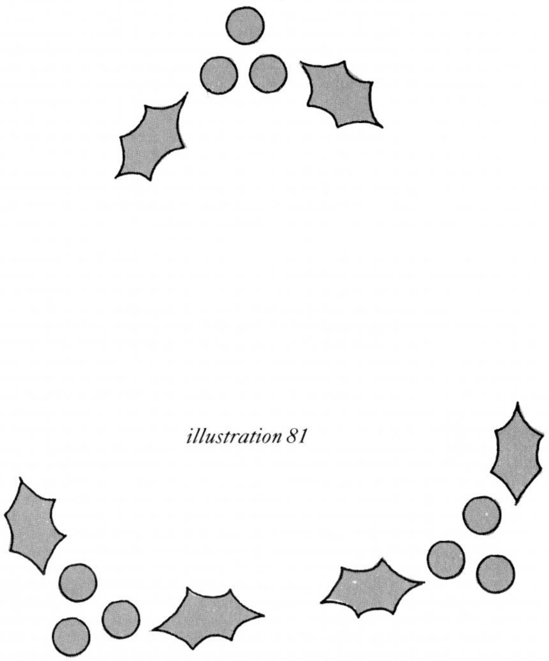

illustration 81

GIFT CERTIFICATES

When an hour of helping in the garden, a trip to the zoo, or a ride in the country would be the perfect gift, just fill in the blanks and give a gift certificate to that special someone.

The following gift certificates may be photocopied or used as a guide for your own. Try using colored paper, or painting borders with touches of watercolor. Gold and silver metallic pens with fine tips are also useful for decorating certificates. Sticker and rubber stamp art are also fun methods of personalizing the certificates.

Try scenting certificates by storing copies in an envelope with lavender or sandalwood.

Permission granted to photocopy this page for personal use only.

GIFT CERTIFICATE

The bearer of this certificate is entitled to

_____

_____

_____

by virtue of being a wonderful

_____!

Enjoy! I love you!

GIFT CERTIFICATE

The recipient of this magic gift certificate is entitled to

_____

_____

_____

because you are the best

_____

that I could ever have!
Enjoy! I love you!

CRAFTER'S LABELS

Personally crafted gifts certainly deserve to be signed by the artist.

hotocopy these labels on white or colored paper. Add a touch of paint or sign with gold ink. Cut out labels and use white craft glue to affix labels to your projects.

For small projects, photocopy label, sign, and run through a copy machine capable of reductions.

Labels can be copied on card stock, a hole punched in the corner, and tied to presents with pretty ribbon.

Permission granted to photocopy this page for personal use only.

GIFT WRAP

Packages wrapped in bluebird paper, all tied in bright ribbons, brown garden twine encircling little gifts in colored tissue...the anticipation of opening presents so beautifully presented is a gift in itself. Gift crafting is not over until we have designed the presentation and topped it with a lovely bow.

rap gifts to fit the mood of the season or a special interest. Experiment with different colors and patterns. Unusual trims and small trinkets add flair and individuality to presents for any occasion.

Ribbon need not be limited to bows. Try knotting, braiding, and twisting; or create roses and leaves with simple rolling and folding techniques. To make a ruffle, pull through one wire of wired ribbon; pull through both wires to create an interesting effect (see page 28).

Berries, flowers and the fruit of each season inspired the wraps designed in the following pages. Instructions are for bows and decorations; papers are listed in the Materials list. As the size and shape of packages will vary, measure your package to determine the quantity of wrapping material that will be necessary. Use the Materials list as a guideline, and add or subtract materials to accommodate your gift box.

The projects in each photograph are listed clockwise from upper right.

Insert fresh violets, jonquils, and sprigs of lilac into florst's tubes with water. Tape tube to package, concealing it with a pretty bow.

Delicate colors delight us and mirror the freshness of the outdoors. Tender greens and hints of yellow and pink begin to show in the garden. All we need to do is look about us to get a flavor of spring.

HATBOX OF RIBBON ROSES

MATERIALS:

One 8x4-inch hatbox (24-inch circumference)

Twenty-six to twenty-eight 18-inch pieces of assorted French wired ribbon

5½ yards of 1½-inch-wide pale aqua French wired ribbon

5 yards of ¼-inch-wide celery antique silk ribbon

⅔ yard of 1-inch-wide green satin ribbon

¾ yard of ¾-inch-wide sage embroidered double-edged ruffle tape

¾ yard of 2-inch-wide Battenberg lace

25x7½-inch rectangle cream-and-dusty-rose striped cotton fabric

Spray adhesive

1 square white felt

Scissors

Glue gun/glue sticks

STEP 1

Glue ¼ inch of satin ribbon to top side of box, folding and gluing remaining width to top and creating a finished edge.

STEP 2

Make 26 to 28 ribbon roses (see page 28). Cut aqua ribbon into 5-inch lengths. To make leaves, form a figure-8 loop with each piece. Glue to underside of each ribbon rose. Glue ribbon roses to box top to cover completely. Position gentle loops of ¼-inch antique silk ribbon on box lid, among roses and leaves. Use dots of hot glue to secure into place.

STEP 3

Apply spray adhesive to fabric rectangle. Center and smooth fabric around box, allowing 2 inches to fold inside box. Fold side seam under and secure with hot glue. Fold excess fabric at both top and bottom and press into place.

STEP 4

Glue embroidered ruffle tape around side of box top. With hot glue, secure lace around top edge of box bottom.

STEP 5

Trace box bottom onto felt square. Cut out, making circle slightly smaller. Glue to bottom of box.

PEACH LADDER BOW

Make a chain of single bows to create a ladder bow for gift wrap (see page 27). Glue bow to a comb or barrette to adorn hair. The ladder bow shown requires 2½ yards of ½-inch-wide ribbon. Tiny ribbon roses are glued into place.

LACE DOILY WRAP

MATERIALS:

One 12-inch round white Battenberg lace doily

¾ yard French wired ribbon, color and width of your choice

Thread ribbon through alternate lace holes in doily. Gather together and tie in a pretty single bow. Trim streamer ends in an inverted "V" shape.

MAUVE RIBBON ROSE

MATERIALS:

4x4-inch square white gift box

2 yards of ½-inch-wide iridescent mauve French wired ribbon

9 green ribbon ferns

Glue gun/glue sticks

Tie mauve ribbon around box and finish with a single knot on center of box top. Wrap ribbon ends around each other in a clockwise direction, tucking ends under rosette. With glue, secure ends. Glue fern ends beneath rosette.

ROSE FABRIC WRAP

MATERIALS:

Blue-and-white striped fabric to wrap box

1 yard of ¼-inch-wide blue cord

3 white silk ribbon roses with green leaves

Scissors

Glue gun/glue sticks

To determine fabric measurements, place box on fabric rectangle and practice folds to determine size of twisted fabric rose.

STEP 1

Center box on wrong side of fabric (see illustration 82). Fold longest sides up and over box (see illustration 83). Edges of fabric will overlap.

STEP 2

Pull remaining long sides of fabric up and toward center, crossing ends (see illustration 84).

STEP 3

Flatten and twist ends around each other. Tuck beneath twist. Ends may be glued to secure.

STEP 4

Tie cord around twist, ending in a single bow with 5-inch streamers (see page 27). Knot ends to prevent them from becoming frayed (see illustration 85).

STEP 5

Glue ribbon roses to decorate.

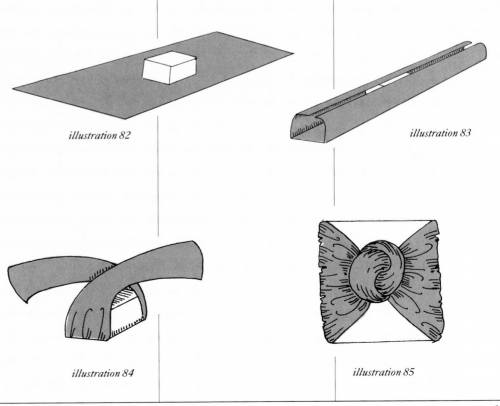

illustration 82

illustration 83

illustration 84

illustration 85

Brightly colored tissue is always appropriate for summer wrapping. Try painting with liquid bleach on tissue using an old brush. Paint tissue on a well-protected surface.

SUMMER GIFT WRAP

Summer parties beneath the oak tree, complete with strawberry ice cream and party dresses, call for gift wraps of flowers.

Imported floral handkerchiefs or squares of hemmed cotton make instant cover-ups for presenting small pots of herbs and flowers. Add lace edging for a sweet Victorian flavor.

SUMMER FLOWERPOT

MATERIALS:

1 standard floral print handkerchief

1 yard of ¼-inch-wide green hand-painted rayon taffeta ribbon

One 4-inch standard flowerpot

Center flowerpot on handkerchief. Pull corners upward to cover pot. Encircle pot with ribbon. Make a pretty double bow with streamers (see page 27).

Accompany your teddy bear gift with chocolates from Amsterdam or small English soaps presented by teddy in a little basket to keep.

TINY GARDEN BASKET

MATERIALS:

1 small basket, natural or painted

Garlands of ribbon flowers

Glue gun/glue sticks

Glue ribbon garlands around small basket twice to decorate.

NOSEGAY FLOWER WRAP

MATERIALS:

A selection of preserved summer flowers: miniature roses, bachelor's buttons, daisies, baby's breath, carnations

Small amount dried fern

¾ yard of ⅝-inch-wide blue handpainted rayon taffeta ribbon

Yellow floral gift wrap

Green florist's tape

8-inch piece florist's wire

Wire cutter

Glue gun/glue sticks

STEP 1

Wrap box in floral paper.

STEP 2

Cut one 2½-inch piece of ribbon and fold over to create a loop. Hold ends firmly against florist's wire, and wrap florist's tape around both until wire is covered.

STEP 3

Arrange ferns and flowers in a small nosegay and glue stems together. Position nosegay on top of ribbon loop, taping stems to wire with florist's tape. Spiral wire end to finish.

STEP 4

Cut remaining ribbon into 3 equal pieces. Form 2 upward-facing loops in front of nosegay to make collar. Tie third piece around loops (see illustration 86). Trim streamer ends and glue to top of box.

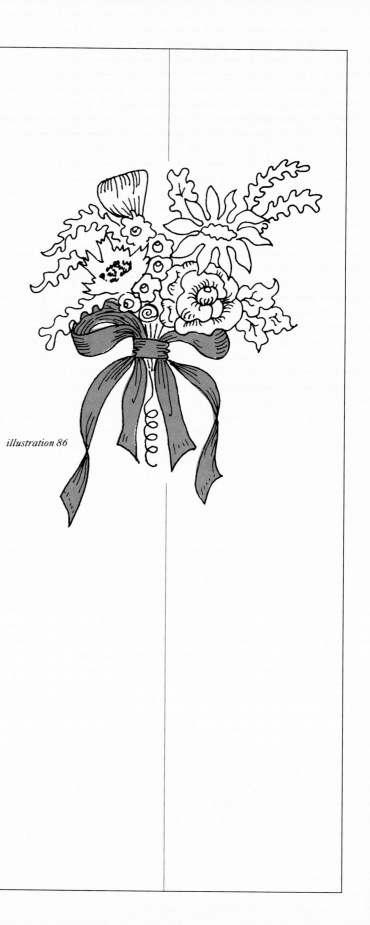

illustration 86

*A simple
way to wrap books
with well-designed
covers is to let the
present speak for itself!
Choose small items
that represent the
book's theme as
accents.*

TEA PARTY WRAP

Present a little book of
English tea recipes with a
tiny cup and saucer. Using
low-melt hot glue, attach
cup to saucer and tie with
ribbon, and you are ready
for a tea party.

AUTUMN GIFT WRAP

Antique tapestries inspired this collection of gift wrap. Harvested fruit and autumn leaves join to speak of the richness and quiet of fall.

AUTUMN COLORS WRAP

MATERIALS:

Fruit print gift-wrap paper

1½ yards of ⅝-inch-wide deep violet French wired ribbon

½ yard of 1-inch-wide rust with green edging French wired ribbon

1 stem artificial grapes

1 slice dried orange

1 sprig dried baby ivy

Glue gun/glue sticks

STEP 1
Wrap package in gift-wrap paper. Wrap violet ribbon around package diagonally (see illustration 87). Trim excess and glue ends. With excess violet ribbon, attach one end to box side and form a cascade of loops trailing onto box top and secure with glue.

STEP 2
Use rust ribbon to tie a single bow, 3 inches wide overall (see page 27). Glue bow to package, overlapping cascade.

STEP 3
Glue grapes and orange slice near center of bow. Glue ivy leaves among grapes.

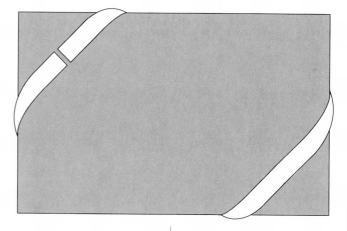

illustration 87

LEAF PRINT BOX

MATERIALS:

1 small brown paper heart box

Metallic copper and metallic deep gold acrylic paint

Plate for spreading paint

Round brush

2 oak leaves (and 2 to 3 extra for testing)

Using round brush, spread individual colors on plate to creamy consistency. Using the following technique, test a few leaves on paper to get the right pressure for printing on box.

STEP 1

Press 1 leaf in deep gold paint, covering entirely. Press painted side of leaf on box top to print. Lift leaf carefully, taking care not to smear paint. Allow paint to dry before proceeding.

STEP 2

Repeat process with second leaf in copper paint.

NESTED SPARROW WRAP

MATERIALS:

Autumn gift-wrap paper

1 yard of 2-inch-wide pale gold organdy ribbon

1 yard of ¼-inch-wide peach antique-silk ribbon

Small mushroom bird in nest

Few sprigs bleached maidenhair fern

Small bunch berries

Small bunch silk flowers

Glue gun/glue sticks

STEP 1

Wrap package in gift-wrap paper. Tie package with organdy ribbon, finishing with a single bow (see page 27).

STEP 2

Glue fern, in a half circle, around nest. Glue a few berries inside nest. With hot glue, secure nest to center of bow.

STEP 3

Glue antique-silk ribbon loops and streamers around nest, opposite ferns. Glue berries and tiny flowers as needed to fill in and add color.

AUTUMN'S RAINBOW

Create an opulent bow to add to autumn gifts of any size by using yellow roses dried from the summer garden and glued into place on a ladder bow of exquisite French ribbon (see page 27). The bow pictured requires 2 yards of 1½-inch-wide French wired ombré ribbon.

WINTER GIFT WRAP

Merry Christmas! Traditional colors of the season, all trimmed with glistening details of gold, wrap presents made so lovingly. Plan an evening, candles glowing, near the fire to wrap presents this year!

CHRISTMAS CLOVER BOW

This versatile bow can be used to adorn large packages, as a Christmas card hanger, or as a holiday picture bow.

MATERIALS:

1 yard of 2-inch-wide Christmas green with gold-edge French wired ribbon

One 3-inch bow-shaped brass charm with streamers

¼ yard of 2-inch-wide gold metallic fringe

Small length florist's wire

Wire cutter

Glue suitable for metal

Glue gun/glue sticks

STEP 1
Cut a 28-inch length of ribbon and fold over 3 inches to form loop. Secure loop with twist of wire (see illustration 88). With

remaining ribbon, form single bow, 4 inches wide overall (see illustration 89). Glue bow to long ribbon on top of wired section (see illustration 89).

illustration 88

illustration 89

illustration 90

STEP 2
Glue charm to center of bow, positioning charm streamers across bow loops.

STEP 3
Fold bottom of streamer to form a "V" shape. Encircle ribbon point with metallic fringe wrapped around several times to create a tassel. Secure end with hot glue.

MEDALLION RIBBON

Decorate box tops or make special gift cards or enclosures by gluing a collage of ribbons and paper medallions.

MATERIALS:

Deep red construction paper

4⅜x1½-inch deep green jacquard-print Christmas ribbon

1 gold Dresden paper medallion

1 silver paper doily

1 gold Dresden paper sunburst cherub medallion

Rectangular white gift box or 5x5-inch square heavy paper, folded lengthwise

White craft glue

Scissors

STEP 1
Glue red paper to box top or heavy paper using white craft glue. Center and glue green ribbon to red paper.

STEP 2
Glue gold medallion to back of sunburst cherub at top. Embellish with sections cut from silver doily.

STEP 3
Glue sunburst cherub medallion to center of green ribbon.

To adapt the Victorian cone wrap to any season simply change the fabric and trims. Collect and dry holly leaves. Paint leaves with a wash of metallic gold acrylic paint and add to your Christmas wrap.

VICTORIAN TREASURE WRAP

MATERIALS:

One 3x3x3-inch Victorian print Christmas box

1 yard of 3-inch-wide Christmas red organdy ribbon

1 yard of ¼-inch-wide scroll braid with green center

Brass charms:

   1 cherub-shaped

   1 star-shaped

   1 bow-shaped

1 filigree bow-shaped

5 craft jewels, 2 blue, 3 red

1 dried holly leaf

1 tiny gold heart bead

Pale metallic gold acrylic paint

Round brush

Glue suitable for metal

Glue gun/glue sticks

STEP 1

Using round brush, paint holly leaf with a wash of gold (see page 33). Set leaf aside to dry.

STEP 2

Using glue suitable for metal, attach several charms and jewels to box, saving filigree bow and one red jewel. Wrap sides of box in organdy ribbon and secure with hot glue. With hot glue, attach a piece of organdy ribbon to cover box lid.

STEP 3

Glue braid around upper and lower edges of box. Form a loop of remaining braid and secure to top corners of box. Pull loop gently to form a "V" shape and glue point to box.

STEP 4

Glue filigree bow to center of braid on front of box. With glue for metal, attach red jewel to center of bow. Glue leaf to far upper-right-hand corner. Glue tiny gold heart to center of leaf.

GREEN-AND-WHITE CHRISTMAS BOX

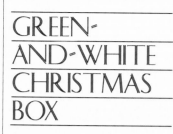

Beautifully presented, simply done...wrappings for small packages can easily be found in a scrapbox. Small prints and stripes combine with bits of ribbon, trim, and ornaments to wrap small gifts instantly.

FOIL RIBBON WRAP

Use wide, printed foil-paper ribbon to wrap small gifts. Paper ribbons will not become frayed, and can be cut to desired widths or fringed.

CHRISTMAS CONE

Here a holiday decoration dating from Victorian times is translated into gift wrap.

MATERIALS:

2 snow cone cups

½ yard Christmas print cotton fabric

1 tassel of 1⅝-inch metallic fringe

½ yard of ¼-inch-wide red and gold braided cord

½ yard of ¼-inch-wide scroll braid with red center

½ yard of ¾-inch-wide metallic gold tassel trim

1 medium Tiffany-style gold button with rhinestones

1 gold Dresden paper medallion

Ruler

Fabric marking pen

Scissors

Spray adhesive

Fabric glue

Glue gun/glue sticks

STEP 1
Carefully open one cone to use as pattern. Place fabric, right side down, on flat surface and position opened cone on it. Using ruler and marking pen draw lines on fabric, allowing 1 inch on each side and 7 inches at top (see illustration 91). Cut out.

STEP 2
Fold over ¼ inch at top of fabric and iron. With fabric glue, secure into place.

STEP 3
Apply spray adhesive to remaining cone, position, and smooth fabric into place. Fold ¼ inch under to finish back seam and glue into place.

STEP 4
Attach tassel trim to top edge of fabric with fabric glue. Glue scroll braid on top edge of tassel trim. Glue paper medallion to front of fabric cone. Glue tassel to fabric cone point.

STEP 5
Place gift in cone. Tie braided cord in a double knot. With hot glue, attach jeweled button to center of knot.

illustration 91

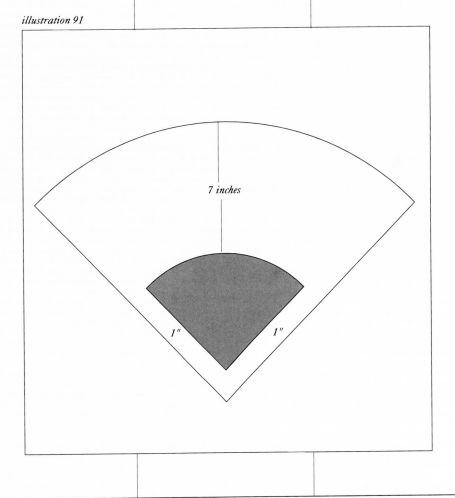

7 inches

1"   1"

RESOURCE GUIDE

❧ Adhesives

Black & Decker Thermogrip
Glue Gun Hot and low-melt glue guns

Loctite Corporation
4450 Cranwood Parkway
Cleveland, OH 44128
(800) 321-9188
Wide range of adhesives

❧ Baskets and Wreaths

Comforts of Home
(800) 44-SMELL
Scented twig products

❧ Blank Canvas Products

Matthew Thomas Designs
8868 Clairemont Mesa Blvd.
Suite A
San Diego, CA 92123
(619) 565-0179
Pillow covers, dolls and more

The Dalee Book Company
267 Douglass Street
Brooklyn, NY 11217
(718) 852-6969
Stationery sets and more

❧ Children's Art Supplies

Binnie & Smith Consumer Information
1100 Church Street
P.O. Box 431 Easton, PA 18004

❧ Decorative Accessories

Albert Kessler & Co.
1355 Market St., Ste. #405
San Francisco, CA 94103-1383
(800) 537-7537
Baskets and porcelain

The Bluebird House at Terra
Route 7, Box 382
Fayetteville, AR 72701
Handcrafted glass bluebirds

Clay City Pottery, Inc.
Box 305
Clay City, IN 47841
(800) 776-2596

Liberty of London
Regent Street
London, SW1 England
Gift-wrap paper, fabric

Michel & Company/Charpente
P.O. Box 3625
Culver City, CA 90231-3625
Fine accessories and paper products

Mills River Industries
824 Locust Street
Hendersonville, NC 28792
Wide range of rugs

Paper Parade
504 Bay Avenue
Capitola, CA 95010
(408) 476-2311
Unique accessories

Risney Bears
Jodee & Dave Risney
3234 Maplethorpe Lane
Soquel, CA 95073
Handmade bears

The Rug Barn
P.O. Box 1187
Abbeville, SC 29620
(803) 446-2170
Wide range of rugs

United Design
P.O. Box 1200
Noble, OK 73068
(800) 727-4883
Wonderful critters

Wisteria Antiques
5870 Soquel Drive
Soquel, CA 95073
(408) 462-2900
French antiques

❧ Dried Botanicals

Jones & Bones Unltd.
621 Capitola Avenue
Capitola, CA 95010
(408) 462-0521
Gourmet herbs and twig pencils

Naturally Herbs
59 Alden Avenue
Warwick, RI 02889
Dried fruits

Naturally Yours
1423 Buckskin Drive
Santa Maria, CA 93454
(805) 922-6184
Freeze-dried flowers

❧ European Specialties

D. Blumchen & Company
P.O. Box 929
Maywood, NJ 07607
Extraordinary items

🍎 Fabric

Benartex,
Inc. New York, NY

Fabric Traditions
1350 Broadway
Suite 2106
New York, NY

Foust Textiles, Inc.
608 Canterbury Road
Kings Mountain, NC 28086
(800) 258-9816
Wholesale only
Fabrics, laces and trims

Peter Pan Fabrics/
Henry Glass & Company
New York, NY

Textra International
Barton Mill
Audlett Drive
Abingdon, Oxfordshire
OX143TZ

🍎 Garden Tools

Fiskars Manufacturing
Corporation
7811 West Stewart Avenue
Wausau, WI 54401
Excellent garden tools

🍎 Notions

Wallflower Designs
1573 Millersville Road
Millersville, MD 21108
Fabric markers

Sulky of America
3113-D Broadpoint Drive
Harbor Heights, FL 33983
Thread and iron-on transfer pens

🍎 Paint

Accent Products Division
HPPG, Borden Inc.
Lake Zurich, IL 60047
All colors, metallics and glue

Delta Shiva
2550 Pellissier Place
Whittier, CA 90601
All colors

Duncan Enterprises
5673 E. Shields Avenue
Fresno, CA 93727
All colors, metallics, and crackle medium

🍎 Paper Products

The Gifted Line
700 Larkspur Landing Circle
Suite 163
Larkspur, CA 94939
Victorian papers

Ivy Imports
5410 Annapolis Road
Bladensburg, MD 20710
Imported marbled paper

Lenz Arts
142 River Street
Santa Cruz, CA 95060
(408) 423-1935
Handmade paper

❧ Potpourri Supplies

Balsam Fir Products
Morse Hill Road
P.O. Box 9
West Paris, ME 04289
(800) 522-5726
Extraordinary potpourri

**Hanna's Potpourri
Specialties, Inc.**
P.O. Box 3647
Fayetteville, AR 72702
(800) 327-9826
Oils and potpourri

Kiehl's
109 Third Avenue
New York, NY 10003
Essential oils

❧ Pressed Flowers and Herbs

**Marty Ryan Herbs &
Herbal Crafts**
22948 Springwell Ct. #207
Novi, MI 48375
(313) 344-9036
Drying racks, flower presses

Tom Thumb Workshops
Route 13, P.O. Box 382
Mappsville, VA 23407
(804) 824-3507
*Pressed flowers, herbs, oils and
accessories*

❧ Ribbons & Trims

All Cooped Up
560 S. State
Orem, UT 84058
(801) 226-1517
Doll hair and accessories

Barrett House
P.O. Box 585
North Salt Lake, UT 84054
(801) 299-0700
Battenberg lace

Creative Beginnings
475 Morro Bay Blvd.
Morro Bay, CA 93442
(800) 642-7238
Victorian charms

Elsie's Esquisiques
513 Broadway
Niles, MI 49120
(800) 742-SILK
Austrian trims, antique ribbons

JHB International
Denver, CO 80231
Buttons

Paulette Knight
343 Vermont Street
San Francisco, CA 94102
French wired ribbon

Lion Ribbon Company, Inc.
100 Metro Way
P.O. Box 1548
Secaucus, NJ 07096
Wired ribbon and more

McGinley Mills, Inc.
Heckman & Bates Streets
Phillipsburg, NJ 08865
Seasonal and wired ribbon

MPR Associates, Inc.
P.O. Box 7343
High Point, NC 27264
(800) 334-1047
Excellent selection paper ribbon

Midori, Inc.
3902 Bagley Avenue N.
Seattle, WA 98103
(206) 547-3913
Fine organdy ribbon

❧ Wood Products

Add Your Touch
Ripon, WI
Birdhouses, small wood products

Designs by Bentwood, Inc.
P.O. Box 1676
Thomasville, GA 31799
Baskets, boxes and trays

Mill Store Products, Inc.
Contact Mark Ferro for
Wholesale Inquiries
New Bedford, MA
(800) 444-7772
Small benches, drying racks and more

INDEX

Joni Prittie